MW01284384

Subscription Business Model: The Ultimate Guide to Building and Scaling A Predictable Recurring Income Business

Attract and Retain Loyal Subscribers, and Maximize Your Profitability with Proven Strategies and Best Practices

By Change Your Life Guru

Books by **Change Your Life Guru**:

Affiliate Marketing Mastery: *The Ultimate Guide to Starting Your Online Business and Earning Passive Income - Unlock Profitable Affiliate Secrets, Boost Earnings with Expert Strategies, Top Niches, High-Performance Products, Innovative Tactics and Essential Tools for Success*

Dropshipping Business Mastery: *The Ultimate Guide to Starting & Managing a Thriving Dropshipping Business - Skyrocket Your Income with Proven Strategies, Profitable Niches, and Unleash Powerful Marketing Tactics*

Etsy Store Mastery: *The Ultimate Guide to Building Your Own Etsy Empire - Learn Proven Strategies for Finding & Selling the Hottest Products, Building Your Brand, and Dominating Your Niche on Etsy*

Online Course Mastery: *The Ultimate Guide to Creating and Marketing Profitable Online Courses - Learn How to Find Your Niche, Create Engaging Content, and Succeed as an Online Course Creator*

Online Freelancing Mastery: *The Ultimate Guide to Making Money as an Online Freelancer - Unlock Proven Strategies to Monetize Your Skills and Talents, Market Yourself, and Go from Zero To Success*

Online Tutoring: *The Ultimate Guide to Creating a Profitable Online Tutoring Business — Become an Expert in Your Niche, Craft Engaging Sessions, Harness Powerful Marketing Strategies, and Profit from Your Expertise in the Digital Learning World*

Print on Demand Mastery: *The Ultimate Blueprint for Print on Demand Success - Unlock Actionable Tips & Strategies to Starting, Setting Up, and Marketing a Profitable Print on Demand Business*

Social Media Influencer: *The Ultimate Guide to Building a Profitable Social Media Influencer Career - Learn How to Build Your Brand, Create Viral Content, and Make Brands Beg to Pay for Your Lifestyle*

Subscription Business Model: *The Ultimate Guide to Building and Scaling A Predictable Recurring Income Business - Attract and Retain Loyal Subscribers, and Maximize Your Profitability with Proven Strategies and Best Practices*

YouTube Influencer: *The Ultimate Guide to YouTube Success, Content Creation, and Monetization Strategies - Build and Grow a Thriving YouTube Channel and Boost Engagement with Proven Techniques and Insider Secrets*

THANK YOU – A Gift For You!

THANK YOU for purchasing our book! *You could have chosen from dozens of other books on the same topic but you took a chance and chose this one.* As a token of our appreciation, we would like to offer you an exclusive **FREE GIFT BOX**. Your Gift Box contains powerful downloadable products, resources and tools that are the perfect companion to your newly-acquired book, and are designed to catapult you towards freedom and success.

To get instant access, just go to:
https://changeyourlife.guru/toolkit

Inside your Free Gift Box, you'll receive:

- **Goal Planners and Schedulers**: Map out manageable and actionable steps so you have clarity and are empowered with a clear roadmap to achieve every goal.

- **Expert Tips & Tricks:** Invaluable tips and strategies ready to apply to your life, or business, to accelerate your progress and reach your outcomes.

- **Exclusive Content:** Free bonus materials, resources, and tools to help you succeed.

- **New Freebies:** Enter your email address to download your free gift box and be updated when we add new Free Content, ensuring you always have the tools, information and strategies to sky-rocket your success!

Are you ready to supercharge your life? Download your gift box for FREE today! [**https://changeyourlife.guru/toolkit**]

Table of Contents

INTRODUCTION.. 1

CHAPTER 1: INTRODUCTION TO THE SUBSCRIPTION BUSINESS MODEL AND
HOW IT WORKS... 7

SUBSCRIPTION SERVICE BUSINESS MODEL EXPLAINED 7
A BRIEF HISTORY OF SUBSCRIPTION SERVICE BUSINESSES................................. 8
MODERN EXAMPLES OF SUBSCRIPTION SERVICE BUSINESSES 10
WHAT SETS APART A SUBSCRIPTION SERVICE BUSINESS MODEL FROM A TRANSACTIONAL
BUSINESS MODEL... 12
TEN BENEFITS OF A SUBSCRIPTION SERVICE BUSINESS MODEL 13
    1. You Get a Predictable Recurring Revenue 14
    2. A Strong Customer Base and Increased Customer Loyalty 14
    3. Flexible Pricing Points 15
    4. Have Better Customer Retention 15
    5. Enhanced Customer Engagement.. 16
    6. Improved Opportunities for Marketing Your Business........................... 16
    7. Improved LTV 17
    8. Enhanced Cash Flow Management 17
    9. Cheaper Cost of Acquiring New Subscribers 18
    10. Easier to Scale... 18
CHECKLIST... 19

CHAPTER 2: TYPES OF SUBSCRIPTION BUSINESS MODELS 21

SAAS SUBSCRIPTION SERVICE BUSINESS MODEL... 21
    Overall Benefits of a SaaS Subscription Business Model............................ 22
    Drawbacks of a SaaS Subscription Service Business Model 23
    How SaaS Subscription Service Businesses Price Their Offerings................ 24
E-COMMERCE SUBSCRIPTION MODEL 25
    A Subscription Box Defined.. 25
    Ten Popular Types of Subscription Boxes... 28
ON-DEMAND CONTENT DELIVERY SUBSCRIPTION SERVICE MODEL 31
    VOD.. 31
MEMBERSHIP-BASED SUBSCRIPTION SERVICE MODEL 33
NON-PROFIT SUBSCRIPTION SERVICE BUSINESS MODEL.................................... 35
CHECKLIST... 36

CHAPTER 3: WHY SOME SUBSCRIPTION SERVICE BUSINESSES FAIL 37

A TRANSPORTATION SUBSCRIPTION SERVICE BUSINESS THAT COLLAPSED....................... 37
A NEW ORLEANS STARTUP VENTURE THAT BURNED $10.5 MILLION OF INVESTOR MONEY 38

TOP FIVE CAUSES OF FAILURE OF SUBSCRIPTION SERVICE BUSINESSES 40
   1. Lack of Novelty *40*
   2. Lack of Clarity About the Target Subscriber *41*
   3. Excluding Your Mission in Your Offering *42*
   4. Inflexible Pricing at the Time of Subscription *44*
   5. Failure to Involve Subscribers *45*
   6. Providing Complex Offers *45*
CHECKLIST 46

CHAPTER 4: HOW TO BUILD A SUBSCRIPTION SERVICE BUSINESS FROM SCRATCH 47

   1. FIND A SUBSCRIPTION IDEA FOR YOUR BUSINESS 47
   2. RESEARCH THE MARKET...49
   3. CREATE A PRODUCT 51
   4. CREATE A VALUE PROPOSITION 53
   5. CREATE SUBSCRIPTION PACKAGES AND PRICING STRATEGY.....................55
      Subscription Pricing Strategies *55*
      How to Set Prices for Your Subscription Service *57*
   6. CHOOSE THE MINIMUM TECHNOLOGY YOU NEED FOR YOUR BUSINESS 59
      Website: Your Main Workhorse *60*
      CMS *60*
      Website Analytics *61*
      Recurring Billing System *62*
      Marketing and Marketing Automation *62*
      Order Management System *64*
      Customer Relationship Management *65*
      Payment Recovery Solution *65*
   7. CRAFT A SALES PAGE FOR YOUR SUBSCRIPTION OFFER 66
      Two Versions of Sales Pages..*66*
      The Main Components of a Sales Page *67*
   8. VALIDATE YOUR SUBSCRIPTION SERVICE BUSINESS IDEA.........................69
   9. ONBOARD YOUR NEW SUBSCRIBERS SEAMLESSLY.................................72
   CHECKLIST 75

CHAPTER 5: HOW TO CONVERT TO A SUBSCRIPTION BUSINESS MODEL FROM A PRODUCT OR SERVICE 77

   WHY DO YOU WANT TO CONVERT TO A SUBSCRIPTION BUSINESS MODEL? 77
   HOW TO EVALUATE YOUR CURRENT BUSINESS MODEL 78
   RESEARCH AND UNDERSTAND YOUR CURRENT CUSTOMERS 81
      Figure Out What Your Customers Want...............................*81*
   WHAT'S THE COMPETITION DOING?..83
   CREATE A VALUE PROPOSITION...84
   ESTABLISHING YOUR PRICING STRATEGY...84
   SELECT THE RIGHT TECHNOLOGY 85

TEST YOUR SUBSCRIPTION SERVICE 85

CHECKLIST.. 86

CHAPTER 6: THE ART AND SCIENCE OF ATTRACTING CUSTOMERS TO YOUR SUBSCRIPTION BUSINESS **87**

SALES FUNNEL: WHAT IT IS AND WHY YOU NEED IT 87

Four Stages of a Sales Funnel 89

The Six-Step Process for Creating Your Sales Funnel 91

How to Measure the Effectiveness of Your Sales Funnel 94

THE BEST METHOD TO GET MORE LEADS INTO YOUR SALES FUNNEL............ 95

Pros and Cons of the Freemium Model...................................... 96

THE MOST POTENT METHOD TO CONVERT LEADS INTO SUBSCRIBERS 97

What an Irresistible Offer Means 97

Strategies for Creating an Irresistible Offer............................... 99

CHECKLIST.. 103

CHAPTER 7: STRATEGIES TO RETAIN SUBSCRIBERS...........................**105**

WHAT IS SUBSCRIBER RETENTION RATE AND HOW DOES IT DIFFER FROM CHURN RATE?. 105

WHAT CAUSES HIGH SUBSCRIBER CHURN RATES? 107

1. Low Level of Subscriber Engagement 107

2. Attracting the Wrong Subscribers.. 108

3. Subscribers Aren't Nailing Their Objectives 108

4. Expired Credit Cards.. 109

5. Service Not Meeting Expectations Anymore........................... 109

WHY RETAIN SUBSCRIBERS IN YOUR SUBSCRIPTION SERVICE BUSINESS 110

Increased Free Marketing... 110

It's Affordable to Retain Subscribers....................................... 112

Improved Return on Investment 113

Retained Subscribers Are a Source of Business Improvement Ideas.......... 113

Higher Subscriber LTV.. 114

HOW TO KEEP ENGAGING YOUR SUBSCRIBERS AND RETAIN THEM 114

Create and Send Your Service's Email Newsletter Frequently 115

Accept Mistakes and Apologize 116

Inform Your Subscribers About Price Changes Timely 117

Capitalize on Subscriber Testimonials and Their Stories............. 118

Create a Community Around Your Subscription Service 118

Create a Personalized User Experience.................................... 119

Create and Regularly Update a Subscriber Communication Calendar 119

Provide an Option to Downgrade 120

CHECKLIST.. 121

CHAPTER 8: HOW TO MEASURE THE FINANCIAL PERFORMANCE OF YOUR SUBSCRIPTION SERVICE BUSINESS **123**

INTRODUCTION TO THE FINANCES OF SUBSCRIPTION SERVICES 123

Understanding a Subscription Service's Income Statement *124*

FORECASTING CASH FLOW IN YOUR SUBSCRIPTION SERVICE BUSINESS 130

The Meaning of Cash Flow and Why You Need to Forecast It...................*130*

Three Top Tips for Accurate Cash Flow Forecasting *135*

CHECKLIST 136

CHAPTER 9: TOP FIVE BEST PRACTICES OF SUCCESSFUL SUBSCRIPTION SERVICE BUSINESSES 137

1. USE STORYTELLING TO ILLUMINATE YOUR BUSINESS'S VALUE 137

2. SIMPLIFY SUBSCRIBER USER EXPERIENCE...138

3. BE WILLING TO IMPROVE YOUR BUSINESS CONTINUALLY 140

4. INCENTIVIZE SUBSCRIBERS 141

5. PROMOTE YOUR SUBSCRIPTION SERVICES REGULARLY..144

CHECKLIST 146

CONCLUSION 147

Introduction

Have you ever asked yourself any of the following questions?

- How do subscription services make money?

- Are subscription services profitable?

- How do subscription services work?

- How do I start a successful subscription service business?

- What's the difference between a subscription service business model and a transactional business model?

- What are the benefits of the subscription service business model?

If you have, then consider this scenario: Imagine that a couple of weeks have passed after you've read this book and you've started implementing what you learned in it. How different would your business life be? You'll have answers to all the questions above. Most importantly, you'll be running a subscription service business and enjoying the many benefits that it offers. You can enjoy these benefits whether you start a subscription service business from scratch or you transition from a transactional business model.

If you're running a traditional business, there are numerous challenges you may be facing. For example:

- **Cash flow and financial management**. Among the many causes of business failure, you'll find cash flow as one of the most common causes. However, this isn't the primary cause of business failure—it's a symptom of foundational problems. At any rate, lack of money to run a business can mean the end of your business.

- **Planning ahead**. No one knows for sure what will happen in the future. However, by planning our tomorrows today, we stand a better chance of succeeding. Think about business financial planning, for instance. It's not a simple matter to create such a plan for transactional businesses as opposed to subscription service businesses. It's the difficulty of planning ahead that contributes to cash flow problems.

That's just a small sample of problems every traditional business can face. The good news is that there's a new approach that helps a great deal to address these problems—the subscription service economy.

It's not an accident that the subscription economy is growing fast. Customers love it or else it wouldn't be growing. Although it has existed for centuries, the subscription economy is growing faster than ever before. Consider the following facts:

- The subscription service business model generates more revenue than the retail sector and the S&P 500 industries combined. We've seen subscription services multiplying their growth five times faster than the retail industry and the combined revenue of the S&P 500 companies. This is exciting news, isn't it? There's more about this economy to know.

- Streaming services are expected to hit $155 billion by the end of 2025 while software-as-a-service (SaaS) is earmarked to hit $370 billion by 2026. These are huge numbers that we can't ignore. Imagine if you could take a 0.05% cut of either of these markets! That means you could be making $77.5 million by 2025 if you venture into the streaming services industry today. That's not a small change.

How can you tap into the subscription economy? All of this begins by acquiring the right knowledge, which means you need the right information and guidance. That's what this book is about and why we have structured it the way we have. Not only are you going to gain the needed information, but you'll also get it in the right order so that it's easy to apply. Here's how we've structured this book and what you'll learn in it:

It starts by taking a background look into subscription services to set up a strong foundation. Included in this are a description of subscription services and their history that dates back hundreds of years. If you're under the impression that subscription services are dated, we provide modern examples of this type of business model. You'll discover what type of industries have already adopted subscription services, including some sectors you may not have considered. This will prove beyond doubt that you can start a subscription service business in almost any industry. To help you decide if this model can work for you, we included 10 of its benefits.

Having learned how beneficial subscription services are, we turn our attention to the types of this kind of business model. You'll discover three broad categories of subscription service business models and five specific ones. The five belong to one or more of these broad categories. For each specific subscription service business model, you'll learn what it is, its advantages, and its disadvantages.

The challenge for any entrepreneur is that their startup may fail to take off. We find that subscription service businesses have failed in the past and others may fail in the future. For this reason, it's necessary to learn why subscription service businesses fail and to avoid doing things that can send your business to an early death. We have provided two examples of startups in different industries that failed, as well as lessons from them. Additionally, you'll learn six top reasons subscription service businesses fail and what to do instead.

Once you've set the foundation, you can start learning how to build your subscription service business. By this time, you should already have an idea of which subscription model you like and why. Starting a subscription service business follows a specific process. You'll learn each of the steps involved and how to accomplish them successfully. The process entails how to come up with a business idea right through to validating it. You'll also discover what technology you need to build a successful subscription service. One of these technology tools include a solution that ensures you improve the chances of getting paid when a subscriber's credit card has expired.

If you already own a business, you don't have to start building a subscription service business from scratch. You can convert some of your products or services into subscriptions. The way to do this is slightly different from when starting from scratch. We explain how to do this in detail, extrapolating on where the process differs from starting a subscription service from ground zero. The main advantage of transitioning to a subscription service is that you already have customers you know very well.

Once you have a subscription service, you have to sell it profitably. Many businesses that struggle with cash flow have problems making enough sales or they battle with managing costs. Sales are what makes businesses successful. With subscriptions, your sales approach aims at optimizing subscriber retention, hence you need strategies that build subscriber-business relationships. To help you make enough sales, we provide two effective strategies: one for generating leads and another for converting leads into subscribers.

Once you have subscribers, attention shifts toward retaining them for as long as possible. Subscriber retention is where the value of subscription services becomes highly conspicuous. You'll discover what subscriber retention means and why you should pay attention to it. Most importantly, we detail strategies you can implement to retain your subscribers and maximize revenue.

You can't run a successful subscription service business without paying attention to its finances. Since the income statement of a subscription service business varies slightly from that of a traditional business, we start by introducing the terminology you'll need to learn and use. Only then do we explain how the income statements of the two types of business models differ. Cash flow is critical for the survival and thriving of any business. Hence, you'll also learn how to make a cash flow forecast so that you don't run out of needed cash.

What you would have learned up to this point will get you started with building your subscription service correctly. To optimize the results you achieve, it's helpful to learn what successful subscription services have found to work well. That's why we conclude the book by giving you best practices to incorporate in your business.

Why are we passionate about writing a book such as this one? We are Change Your Life Guru and our aim is to help people like you live more enriched lives. It's for this reason that we strive to write practical books like *Subscription Business Model: The Ultimate Guide to Building and Scaling A Predictable Recurring Income Business*. With this book, we aim to make it simple to start a subscription service business from scratch or to transition to one if you already own a business. The language we use is simple so that you don't have to struggle to implement the ideas we suggest.

We hope that you can decide to join the subscription economy and have a share of its market. Not only will this transform your life, but it will add to the estate of your family. Imagine it's 10 years from now and you've succeeded in building a subscription service business. Instead of worrying about cash flow, you can forecast much more accurately. You never have to worry about running out of cash to pay your business bills and most importantly, your employees are excited to work for your business.

The quickest way to get to that promised land is to decide today to be the most knowledgeable person when it comes to subscription services. This book introduces you to this type of service and helps you build the right foundation for a hugely scalable business. Don't wait a minute longer to decide to start building your knowledge account. Start reading this book right away, beginning with understanding the background of subscription services in Chapter 1.

Chapter 1:
Introduction to the Subscription Business Model and How It Works

The foundation is the crucial part of knowing any new concept or idea. The same goes for the subscription service business model. We need to know what it is, why it's important, how it works, and also its origin. You'll learn all this in this chapter, beginning with discovering what a subscription service business model is.

Subscription Service Business Model Explained

I'm sure you're familiar with the regular business model. You go to a store, online or offline, and purchase a product and never hear from them again. Even many medical professionals operate their businesses in this fashion. Little do they know that their businesses could be much easier if they converted it into a subscription-based business. With that said, you're probably wondering exactly what a subscription service business model is.

Instead of selling one-off products and services, a subscription service business charges its customers a regular fee to continue receiving its services or products. The most popular subscription service business is based on what's known as the subscription box. I'll get into the details of this business model in the next chapter. Essentially, a subscriber receives a box containing various products on a regular basis in exchange for an upfront fee. To keep receiving this box, a subscriber must pay the agreed upon fee, which could be weekly, monthly, annually, or whatever frequency.

Subscribers don't have to stay with a given business, as they can cancel the subscription whenever they want. Since the loss of subscribers is one of the biggest reasons for poor cash flows, subscription service businesses have to focus on subscriber retention. Attracting new customers might be exciting for marketers but it's a costly process. The reason for retaining subscribers is it allows the business to receive recurring income.

Typically, a subscription service business sells products that are needed regularly, such as cleaning products or deodorants. It should be something, a product or service, that the subscriber will need on a regular basis. A closer look at this type of business reveals that it doesn't really sell a product but a service. Most often, subscription businesses sell convenience.

A Brief History of Subscription Service Businesses

In the early to mid-17th century, King Charles I of England approved a patent for a fire insurance scheme. Fires were common in those days, and it was thought that the scheme would financially protect individuals who lost their properties to fire. Interested individuals were expected to subscribe to the scheme the same way we do with most types of insurance, such as auto insurance. The scheme didn't take off since few understood it. Nonetheless, this idea seeded the development of subscription service businesses.

Three decades later, the subscription business model cropped up in the insurance industry and in trading companies. Not long after came book clubs, an idea by publishers and to a lesser degree, authors. Their aim was to get interested people to subscribe to publications that were in the pipeline. In this way, publishers and authors built relationships with readers and were able to sell their publications in large numbers.

Still in the 17th century, subscriptions found their usage in education. Universities advertised their lectures in newspapers and made subscription offers to those interested in gaining or improving their knowledge. Adoption of the subscription business model continued and by the 20th century, it became common practice to subscribe to newspapers and magazines. Prior to that, this model had become valuable for some European countries in ensuring citizens received clean water and vegetables.

The 20th century is the period when the subscription business really took off. Remember that it was during this period that entrepreneurs like Henry Ford perfected the automobile. We can't forget the invention of the aircraft by the Wright brothers. These improvements in transportation improved the logistics area of businesses' value chains. Subscriptions also improved, going from annual subscriptions to monthly, and in some cases, to weekly versions.

An industry that took subscriptions to another level in the 20th century was the media and publishing sector. One of the most popular subscription businesses in the publishing arena is the Book of the Month (BOTM), originally known as Book of the Month Club (BOMC). This business was founded by an advertising copywriter known as Harry Sherman. BOMC hand-selected books that subscribers could purchase and receive monthly. This business still exists today, although in a different format.

In the 1970s, Charles Dolan, founder of HBO and Cablevision, turned the television industry on its head. His idea of TV subscriptions was born out of frustration—cable TV fed viewers limited content to fit in third-party advertisements. Dolan created HBO to provide viewers with content—specifically, movies from Hollywood—in exchange for a monthly fee. Viewers were spared from the influx of advertisements. That was the birth of pay-TV.

October 19, 1985, saw the opening of the first Blockbuster video store. With thousands of video cassettes to choose from, the store instantly became a hit with consumers. To rent a video cassette, you had to fork out a rental fee, deposit, and shipping and handling fees. In the unfortunate event that you returned the cassette late, you were slapped with a late fine. At any rate, Blockbuster opened its 1,000th store in America in the 1990s and started expanding internationally. Instead of video cassettes, Blockbuster was renting out digital video discs (DVDs).

Meanwhile, in 1997, Reed Hastings and Marc Randolph founded Netflix to operate the same way as Blockbuster, with one exception. It operated online instead of running physical stores. After about five years, Netflix adopted a flat-fee subscription business model and later added various subscription plans. If you aren't living under a rock somewhere in the jungle, you know what impact this entertainment juggernaut has had on the world.

The subscription business model sprung to new heights when it became clear in the 1990s that software would change the world. The first subscription-based businesses in this space were application service providers (ASP). With this solution, a subscriber could access a selected set of computer applications over a network. Although ASP didn't succeed, it paved the way for the modern software-as-a-service (SaaS) subscription model. We'll revert to this shortly with more details. It wasn't until the mid-2000s that subscription boxes became the talk of the town. Today, nearly every business can be turned into a subscription service business and generate recurring and predictable income.

Modern Examples of Subscription Service Businesses

It's not only the software technology, media and entertainment, and e-commerce industries that have adopted the subscription service business model. Who would have thought the auto industry could one day incorporate this money-making model into their businesses? Indeed, there are many other industries that have added this business model. We give examples of industries that have adopted this model below:.

- **Vehicle subscription service business model**. Auto subscriptions are available from carmakers like Nissan, rental companies like Hertz, or independent multi-brand companies like Subscribe With Enterprise. The biggest benefit for consumers is that they don't have to spend hefty amounts of money to buy a vehicle. Instead, they can "own" it for a couple of months and switch to another make if they wish. Or, they may choose to subscribe for a given period to use the car for their needs and cancel the subscription thereafter.

One of the automakers that has adopted the subscription service business model is Porsche. You can drive a luxurious Porsche of your choice each month for a fraction of its purchase price. If you don't drive the allotted mileage in a given month, the remaining mileage rolls over into the next month. Your 30-day or 90-day subscription includes insurance, roadside assistance, concierge services, and vehicle maintenance.

- **Fitness subscription service business model**. Tell someone how fun and easy it is to reach their fitness goals and they'll probably laugh at you. When you talk about fitness, people imagine being in a well-equipped gym or a person running nonstop for hours. These images are what motivational speakers use to convince us that becoming fit is hard work. No one ever tells us that when we're walking to a class we love, we're actually exercising. No one tells us that when we're gardening, we're exercising.

Without a way to prove to yourself that you're working out, you can't silence these people. Along came fitness trackers like Fitbit with the right technology to show you that fitness is the sum total of all your minute-to-minute or hour-to-hour activities. All it takes is wearing a fitness tracker that tracks all your activities, from walking to gym or pacing at work. To get the most out of your fitness tracker, it's worth subscribing to a premium fitness plan developed by one of the developers of these trackers. You will receive regular fitness and health-related lifestyle advice with your subscription to keep you on track.

- **Home repair subscription service business model**. There are two ways to approach home repairs: reactive and proactive repairs. The first handles equipment or appliance repairs after they have broken down, while the second handles similar repairs before a piece of equipment goes down. Which of these approaches do you prefer? Although the answer is based on your needs, many people like the second option because their equipment stays operational for longer. This means that they can use it at almost any time they want.

This is where subscriptions come in with home maintenance subscription services. A subscriber can join to receive annual home inspections. Parts for standard equipment, including batteries and filters, can be included in the subscription. With this service, members don't have to wait for a piece of equipment to break down before fixing it. Some of the home equipment can be expensive to repair once they go out of order, however, subscribers can avoid these expensive costs.

There are many other examples of subscription service businesses in a variety of industries. Some common industries include:

- Airline industry

- Gaming

- Education, learning, and development

- Food industry

The message is clear: You can create a subscription service business in almost any industry and niche.

What Sets Apart a Subscription Service Business Model From a Transactional Business Model

It may appear that the difference between a subscription service business model and a transactional one is how income is generated. Although we agree, there's an underlying reason why a subscription service business succeeds. It generates a predictable and recurring income because of its intense focus on customer service and customer experience.

A transactional business tends to worry about making a sale. Imagine you went to a local grocery store and bought bread, cheese, sugar, and tea. If the store is a traditional one, store employees are more likely to worry about you stealing than ensuring that you get what you want. It's very unlikely that someone will show interest in you as a person. No one will ask you how your grandmother, sister, or brother is doing. The reason is that they're not interested in you; rather, they are focused on getting your money. Little do they know that the money is not in the products they sell but in the relationship they build with you.

Once they make the sale, they don't care much about what happens afterward. Questions like "Did the customer receive the best service?" and "Did the product or service deliver the results that the customer wanted?" barely enter into the sales equation. This is exactly the opposite of the approach to sales by subscription service businesses.

The sale in a subscription service business isn't even a product or service; it's a method to start the subscriber-business relationship. It's at that point that the subscription business tries to understand the subscriber for one sole reason: to provide unparalleled value to them. This is at the center of successful subscription businesses. Don't get us wrong; subscription service businesses are in it for the money. However, they see money as a reward, not the end in itself. Isn't this how every business or employee should approach what they do?

Transactional businesses want to make more sales and this can happen if they continue to attract new customers or keep them longer. To build customer loyalty—which helps keep customers longer—transactional businesses have to change their mindset about their customers. It's this mindset that separates successful subscription service businesses from successful transactional businesses. Throughout this book, our aim is to help you develop this kind of mindset.

Ten Benefits of a Subscription Service Business Model

Are you convinced that a subscription service business model is better than a transactional business model? Perhaps you still have some doubts. Well, I'm about to provide you with 10 of the most powerful reasons why you may like this business model. Let's get started with the first one.

1. You Get a Predictable Recurring Revenue

If receiving a regular and predictable income sounds great, you can't go wrong with a subscription business model. With this model, once you capture a customer and provide them with what they want, they stay with you for the long-term. It's hard to find such customers in regular businesses.

Think about how you make purchases of regular items like groceries. Do you shop from the same store monthly or do you shift from store to store? Many people shop around for bargains when they buy groceries. With the increased online shopping for groceries—increasing by 52.9% from 2019 to 2020—we can expect consumers to shop around more stores. For regular businesses, it would be hard to keep customers and generate predictable sales from them.

This is different with subscription service businesses. With retention rates anywhere between 40% and 45%, subscription service businesses are great at delivering recurring and predictable income.

2. A Strong Customer Base and Increased Customer Loyalty

Buyers in subscription-based businesses buy multiple times at a given company. Since these types of businesses are focused on customer service, a customer who buys more than once is likely to have enjoyed their buying experience the first time. As a result, it's much easier to build long-term relationships with such buyers.

One of the techniques subscription-based businesses use, is making customers a part of their community. A feeling of belonging is one of the most powerful psychological needs that humans have. It makes us feel important.

3. Flexible Pricing Points

The focus of subscription-based businesses is to play the long game. This means that they don't push to make a profit from every transaction. This is where the concept of the lifetime value (LTV) of a customer becomes handy. LTV tells you how much a subscriber is worth over the period they buy from you. A business with a lucrative LTV can afford to start its new subscribers at low entry price points. For example, a subscriber could be offered a free subscription box to get the relationship going.

To a layman, this offer might seem as if the business is losing money. It may be so in the short term, but the business knows from its calculations of LTV and up-to-date subscriber data that it'll turn a profit from that customer over a given period of time. I'll illustrate how LTV works elsewhere in this book.

Offering bargains to the right customers is a great way to entice subscribers to start a customer-business relationship with you. Fortunately, subscription-based businesses know this and overcome it by providing unparalleled customer service. If they don't, they know that they're going to lose money over the long-term due to attrition.

The biggest advantage bargains offer, is that you have to do minimal work to attract new subscribers. Not surprisingly, you'll likely spend less on marketing and sales than comparable traditional businesses. Less spending, as you know, can translate to good profits.

4. Have Better Customer Retention

I've touched on this above, but this is such an important benefit that it should stand by itself. It's hard work to attract a customer to your business. Moreover, it costs a lot of money, making it necessary to make it worthwhile. It's estimated that you can spend about 5–25 times more to acquire a customer than to retain one. There's no better way to make the best of customer acquisition than by retaining customers. Most importantly, by retaining customers, you can rocket up your profits between 25% and 95%.

A subscription business makes the best of its customer acquisition cost by keeping regular contact with its subscribers. For example, a food business could share fresh recipes with its subscribers every third day or weekly. Those won't just be recipes, but a strategy to get customers to use its products and demand its services more. Other strategies could include offering rewards for buying a certain group of food products.

These efforts decrease what's called customer or subscriber churn rate—how fast a business loses relationships with its customers or subscribers. A lower churn rate means higher customer retention, and usually a high LTV.

5. Enhanced Customer Engagement

The cornerstone of the subscription business model is customer relationships. The reason for this is that customer relationships build trust. A survey revealed that 81% of both business-to-business (B2B) and business-to-customer (B2C) don't buy from businesses they don't trust. In the same survey, 89% of customers said they'll stop buying from a business that devalues their trust. This tells you how valuable trust is for a business, whether B2B or B2C. Customers who stay with you trust you and find value in what you offer.

There are many ways of engaging with subscribers to build trust, including blog articles, email marketing, newsletters, and social media. What's key, however, is sharing useful information. Check what top marketers do to build trust. All of them use email marketing to serve their email subscribers. They're not afraid to give away some of their best work to their email subscribers. For instance, some give away books, long audio and video interviews, or a list of detailed case studies for free. Most importantly, they keep in touch with their subscribers almost the same way that subscription-based businesses do.

6. Improved Opportunities for Marketing Your Business

Closely linked with enhanced customer engagement are improved opportunities for marketing your business. You may already know that you can increase your business's revenue by getting more new customers, increasing the frequency of customer purchases, or charging higher prices. When you've built trust with your subscribers, you have many chances to upsell or cross-sell as often as possible. This results in your subscribers buying more and more often from you, and thus increasing your revenue.

Suppose that you've built trust with your subscribers. When you share valuable content through an email, your subscribers will believe most (if not all) of what you say. If you include an offer for a product or service, several of them may buy, even if the product or service is from a third party. This is particularly true in the modern world of online purchases where customers research products, services, and brands before they buy.

Direct response marketers have known the power of offering valuable information for many years. What they did, and still do, was provide content they knew their target market wanted and make an offer at the end of the letter or newspaper article. The same principle still works today whether online or offline, which is why it's a key element of a successful subscription-based business.

7. Improved LTV

LTV measures how much your subscriber or customer is worth to you over the period they do business with you. The reason LTV is a better metric for subscriptions than the initial purchase price of a product or service is that a subscriber stays with you longer. Most importantly, they sometimes begin the subscriber-business relationship without paying a dime or purchasing at a huge discount.

Because subscribers typically stay longer in a subscription business, the LTV is higher. How high depends on the quality of the relationship the business has with the subscriber.

8. Enhanced Cash Flow Management

The revenue that subscriptions generate tends to be predictable, which means cash flow is also stable. With this predictability comes your ability to manage your cash. This is crucial for your business because improved cash flow management will bring these benefits:

- You'll rarely run out of money because of improved financial planning.

- Your employees will be paid on time, which in turn, will help your business deliver the required level of customer service and engagement.

- It'll be easier to grow your business, potentially without taking out large loans.

9. Cheaper Cost of Acquiring New Subscribers

As stated earlier, a business can spend 5–25 times more to acquire a new customer than it costs to keep an existing one. For subscription businesses, the cost of bringing in new subscribers tends to be lower because they make irresistible offers upfront. This means that for the same amount of dollars, a subscription business can attract more subscribers than a traditional business.

Subscription businesses can afford to make attractive upfront offers because they play the long game. They know that they'll recoup their money in due time while traditional businesses have to make back their money fast.

10. Easier to Scale

Businesses usually grow by increasing the number of products or services they sell. The reason for this is that the sale of a given product or service can plateau over a period of time. As a result, it can be hard to grow your business. The ability to add new products and services without spending an arm and a leg makes subscriptions attractive. It's this ability to add new products and services that allows subscriptions to innovate and to scale.

With the basics of a subscription business covered, we now turn our attention to options you have when creating subscriptions. This is covered in the next chapter.

Checklist

	Determine what industry and niche you'd like to start a subscription service for.
	Decide what your reasons are for starting a subscription service.
	Determine what value you can add to your customers, for example sending free PDF guides or ebooks.

Chapter 2:
Types of Subscription Business Models

Knowing the ins and outs of a subscription service business isn't enough to enable you to start one. It's possible to choose a type that doesn't suit your business idea. This means you should first learn about the different types of subscription service business models. These models are broadly categorized into curation, replenishment, and access subscription business models. Curation accounts for 55% of the subscription models while replenishment and access make up 32% and 13% of the market, respectively.

In this chapter, the idea is to focus on specific subscription service business models, and not on broad categories. The reason is that we want you to be able to apply what you learn within a short time. We'll explore software-as-a-service (SaaS), e-commerce, on-demand content delivery, membership-based, and non-profit subscription models.

SaaS Subscription Service Business Model

There are numerous examples of successful SaaS subscription service businesses, including video creators, email marketing software, and cloud storage companies. What's common among these applications is that a subscriber pays a periodic fee to access software services. Instead of owning the software, the user accesses it online. SaaS subscription falls into the category of access subscription business model.

It's easy to confuse SaaS with software licensing. When you license software, you pay a one-time fee and access it perpetually. Additionally, you install the software on your computer's hard drive. Many licensed software packages provide users with the right to use the software and exclude support and maintenance. This means that you need to pay additional fees to receive these services. In contrast, SaaS subscriptions bundle access with maintenance and remote customer support.

Overall Benefits of a SaaS Subscription Business Model

A SaaS subscription service business model offers pros and cons to both subscribers and service providers. Before you decide if this business model suits your business idea, you should be aware of them.

- **Users can try the software or offer at no cost**. Many SaaS businesses offer free trials to those who want certainty before they buy. Trial periods vary from 7 to 30 days. During the trial, a subscriber can test if the software does what's promised and suits them. These trials also benefit the service providers because they make it easier to attract new subscribers. This helps a great deal by aiding such businesses with a consistent generation of potential customers.

- **Offers user flexibility**. It's not unusual for a SaaS business to have subscribers with varying financial situations. With tiered offerings common in SaaS business, this accommodates many types of consumers. Moreover, subscribers can choose to upgrade, downgrade, or cancel their subscriptions as they see fit. The choice of product features also adds flexibility, as a subscriber can pay only for what they need.

- **Minimizes expenses for users**. Many years ago, you'd need to fork out hundreds or thousands of dollars to purchase a permanent software license. The problem with this approach was that the user had to keep spending this money due to the rapid change in technology. As you can imagine, this was costly to users. Moreover, it provided minimal flexibility. In contrast, SaaS subscriptions provide users with what they need at a fraction of the cost of buying a permanent license. Additionally, you can access upgrades and other perks without incurring an additional cost.

- **Subscribers receive better data security**. Subscriber data security is paramount for any SaaS provider. Many of these providers allow subscribers to store and back up their data online and access it when needed. The development and advances in cloud computing help with data security through tools such as multifactor authentication.

- **Allows continuous innovation to stay current in software developments.** A SaaS service provider can upgrade their software as fast as is practical. This helps it stay current, competitive, and continue to provide needed subscriber features. Because subscribers can access new software versions faster, service providers have no reason not to refine their offerings regularly. Even in cases when the software mal-performs due to bugs, it's easy to fix them.

Drawbacks of a SaaS Subscription Service Business Model

The SaaS subscription service business model has cons in addition to the advantages discussed above. You need to be aware of these shortcomings so that you can guard against them and protect your business. The main ones we will discuss are that the SaaS subscription service business model is easy to imitate, has a low barrier to entry, is exposed to internet security risks, has a longer sales funnel, and uses complex analytics. Let's briefly expand on each of these drawbacks:

- **It's an easy-to-imitate business model.** For one SaaS business that succeeds, many others try to follow in its footsteps. Although this can happen with any other business model, it's much more pronounced with SaaS businesses. The reason is that it's easier to start compared to a traditional brick-and-mortar version. For example, if a SaaS business finds an effective marketing strategy or sale strategy, others can copy it easily. All they need to do is study the strategy by navigating the successful business's strategy on the web.

- **Longer conversion duration from prospect to a subscriber.** Many SaaS businesses offer free trials to entice prospective customers into trying their product. It's exciting that as much as 66% of subscription service businesses convert 25% of free trialists into subscribers. How long it takes to convert potential subscribers will depend on whether you're running a business-to-customer (B2C) or business-to-business (B2B) venture. Typically, free trials can go as high as 30 days but other SaaS companies offer as little as seven-day trials. Still, it can take up to three months for a prospect to convert into a subscriber. This means you should implement follow-up strategies after the prospect has exhausted their free trial and has not signed up.

- **It operates in a highly competitive industry**. Many businesses have spotted the value of SaaS, which has led to almost every industry adopting this business model. For this reason, it's easy for subscribers to move their money from one business to another. This means that you'll need to have a strong competitive advantage to succeed. Most often, your most effective competitive advantage will hinge on how well you provide customer service.

- **Exposed to security threats**. All who use the internet run the risk of losing data or being attacked by cyber thieves. A SaaS business may fall victim to these threats and expose its subscriber information, such as credit card details, to criminals. It's therefore essential for a software provider to keep the security of its subscriber information at the top of its mind.

- **Uses complex business and marketing analytics**. It's rare to find a single software tool that offers all the marketing and business analytics you need. As a result, you'll use various marketing and business automation tools. The higher the number of data sources you have, the higher the number of silos your business has. This occurs because your data sources might be loosely integrated. As a result, it is harder to have a comprehensive view of your business and marketing analytics.

How SaaS Subscription Service Businesses Price Their Offerings

SaaS subscription service companies can bill subscribers by using any of the methods discussed in Chapter 1. It's not unusual for them to combine their choice of pricing model with either charging based on the number of users or subscriber usage of services.

Combining a pricing model with the number of users that have access to a given account results in what's called a pay-per-seat model. This means that as the number of users per account increases, the subscription fee also rises. Pricing subscriptions this way works well if you have one account that allows other users to have personal access. The drawback of this pricing approach is that costs can escalate quickly as the number of users and their needs increase. Using this approach depends on the kind of product that you have.

You can also charge your subscribers based on their usage of your software, a pricing approach often called usage-based pricing. This is great for subscribers because they use and pay only for what they value. SaaS companies such as payment processors and website hosting providers often use this approach because it makes sense for them. Email marketing companies also tend to use this approach. For example, they usually allow their subscribers to send a certain number of emails for a fixed fee. Once the subscriber sends more emails than this number allows, they incur an additional fee. The big drawback of this approach is the subscriber's usage of the product might be inconsistent, and so it can be hard to predict your revenue.

E-Commerce Subscription Model

The second type of business model applies to the retail industry and is commonly called the e-commerce subscription model. Unlike the SaaS model, this one applies when you sell physical products. There are two main approaches within this model: replenishment and curation models. All of these models or approaches are based on the subscription box. Before we explore replenishment and curation approaches, let's first understand subscription boxes.

A Subscription Box Defined

You can start a retail business based on a subscription box. This allows you to ship multiple products to your subscribers regularly, such as weekly or monthly. You can ship a variety of products in a subscription box, including coffee, health supplements, and laundry products. Your subscribers pay recurring fees in exchange for a delivered subscription box.

There are three key elements in many subscription box services: recurring payments, recurring deliveries, and themed boxes. We don't need to explain recurring payments as we've already done so in Chapter 1. Recurring deliveries are possible provided a subscriber pays an agreed upon recurring subscription fee. Subscribers are attracted to subscription boxes mainly because they buy at discounts to regular prices. For example, the individual products within a subscription box may retail for $200 but sell for $160 through a subscription.

Inside a subscription box, you may include samples of new products you believe will be helpful for your subscribers. This is a cost-effective method for doing market research on new products. Additionally, you can use them to get subscribers to try products they haven't bought before. Product sampling has been a great method for selling products since the 1850s. You can add samples of products in your subscription box to lower your subscriber acquisition costs.

Typically, each subscription features a particular theme that connects the products it contains. This theme can turn out to be a competitive advantage for a subscription business. For instance, you may create a sustainable goods theme to connect with subscribers who're concerned about the environment. The key with theme-creation is to ensure that it resonates with your potential and current subscribers, which is where the market research completed earlier comes in handy.

We now turn our attention to replenishment and curation varieties of e-commerce subscription models because of their importance in the retail industry.

- **Replenishment subscription model**: This model, also called the consumables subscription or subscribe and save model, is most popular when you sell products that subscribers want regularly. Typical products that fall into this category include medicines, food items, laundry items, and health supplements. The good news is that consumers need these types of goods weekly or monthly.

Consumers like replenishment subscription models because they offer convenience. Once they subscribe, they put in nearly zero effort to have the products delivered to their homes. There's no need to worry about placing orders or recalling which brand they previously ordered. Many consumers want their products delivered soon after they've placed orders. When you know that a given subscriber has subscribed to your box, you can deliver their products quickly.

For subscription service businesses, this model can give them a competitive edge over competitors who don't offer subscriptions. This means subscription service businesses can have a bigger share of the market. The other benefits for retailers have been discussed already in Chapter 1.

- **Curation subscription model**: This model relies heavily on the element of surprise to get and keep subscribers. When using this model, your subscribers have no clue what their box will include each time they receive it. Curiosity is a big component of attracting and keeping customers or subscribers. For instance, a catchy title like *"How to Win Friends and Influence People"* triggers human curiosity and nudges us to want to find out what we can do to make friends and also influence them.

The curation subscription model takes advantage of this human attribute. A business that uses it puts together an assortment of products and delivers them to customers. That's why the key attribute of such a business should be continuous innovation. Additionally, this business requires a better understanding of your audience to offer a high level of personalization. Products suited to this type of subscription model include toys, books, wine, and liquor.

When using the curation subscription model, you can easily influence your subscribers to try new products. Part of the reason is that when subscribers sign up, you ask them questions whose responses help you understand their tastes and preferences. Knowing this, you can send your subscribers products that tick the boxes of their wants and needs.

There are few approaches that ensure you hit your subscribers' nerves more so than showing them that you understand and value them. This means that as long as you keep delivering valued customer experiences, you'll achieve and retain subscribers for longer. Most importantly, your business will generate an increased number of referrals, which helps lower CAC.

Ten Popular Types of Subscription Boxes

You can create subscription boxes for nearly any consumable product. However, some types of consumables are more suited to this model, which is why they're popular. Below, we briefly describe 10 of these loved types of subscription boxes:

1. **Clothing subscription boxes**. Clothes aren't consumables, which means that clothing subscription boxes can be used in the curated or access models. Some retailers combine the curated model with access. In this case, a subscriber pays a monthly recurring fee to receive a curated box. Once they receive the box, they choose to pay and keep some of the clothes. The remaining clothes are returned to the retailer.

2. **Food subscription boxes**. Subscribers can subscribe to food subscription boxes that contain foods of their choice. For example, they can subscribe to receive snacks, groceries, or meat boxes. These boxes can be a great source of additional revenue for food retailers who sell in physical stores.

3. **Beauty subscription boxes**. The US beauty industry is gigantic. Its compounded annual growth rate (CAGR) is 2.60% over the 2023–2027 period. It's estimated that this market will be worth $91.41 billion in 2023, which translates to $271.50 per person. Beauty subscription boxes tap into this market, especially because 36.6% of 2023 total revenue will come from online sales. Personal care has become a huge industry, particularly the makeup part. This makes the beauty subscription box a potential source of income for someone interested in the beauty industry.

4. **Coffee subscription boxes**. The coffee industry might not be as huge as the beauty sector, but it can be profitable. There are people who prefer to drink certain types of coffee and don't mind enjoying them daily. If coffee-making is right up your alley, starting a coffee subscription box might be for you. You don't need to be a coffee connoisseur to get into the coffee industry, but be willing to learn and serve your subscribers.

5. **Shaving supply subscription boxes**. Through this box, you can supply razor blades and grooming products to people who see it as a chore to search and find supplies they want. Since users have to purchase grooming supplies numerous times a year, you'll help them save time and effort if you could create a shaving supply and grooming products subscription box. The good news is that you don't even need to have a warehouse since you can drop-ship the boxes directly to your subscribers. This means that your profit margins can be better than that of similar brick-and-mortar businesses.

If you would like to learn more about Dropshipping, why not take a look at our book, ***Dropshipping Business Mastery: The Ultimate Guide to starting and managing a thriving dropshipping business.***

6. **Pet subscription boxes**. Do you love pets? Creating pet subscription boxes might be a way to enter the subscription industry market. Pet owners need consistent supplies of various pet products, including toys, food, and medicine. Providing pet subscription boxes allows pet owners to focus their energies on taking care of their pets.

7. **Book of the month subscription boxes**. Every writer dreams of seeing their name on the bestseller list. One of the methods to hit that status is having their book chosen to be part of a successful book of the month subscription box. This gives them exposure to more readers and possibly increased sales. Book of the month subscription boxes are highly curated, giving subscribers some variety in their reading material. Whatever genres your potential subscribers are interested in, you can curate a subscription box they love.

8. **Toys subscription boxes**. Did you know that as much as 60% of adults buy toys online? The fact that the US is the largest importer of toys should make you pay attention and think about how to have a share of that market. It shouldn't come as a surprise that this industry injected 100 billion dollars into the US economy in 2021. Considering that children are born daily, toys will always be needed. Toy subscription boxes can be a way to tap into this industry. One of the areas you could focus your boxes on could be in education and development.

9. **Hand-made goods subscription boxes**. This is another type of subscription box you may consider starting. The US hand-crafted goods market grew to $241.1 billion in 2021. It's estimated that it'll hit $429.3 billion by 2027, meaning that its growth rate during the 2022–2027 period would be 10.14%. If you are into hand-made goods or can source them, you can cut a piece of this market for yourself. Target audiences, like small businesses, can use hand-made goods to market themselves. With more than 30 million small businesses in the US, you can have a sizable market size without even considering individuals.

   Or If you are considering selling on Etsy and you would like to learn more after you have completed this book, why not take a look at our book, *Etsy Store Mastery: The Ultimate Guide to Building Your Own Etsy Empire.*

10. **Wine subscription boxes**. If you love wine, you can monetize that interest by starting a wine subscription box. Not only do these boxes serve as sources of new wines but also provide important knowledge. For example, subscribers can learn which food items to pair with certain wines.

The list of subscription boxes presented above isn't exhaustive. You can create a subscription box for many different items and focus on certain themes. The types of subscription box you start can only be limited by your imagination.

On-Demand Content Delivery Subscription Service Model

One of the oldest forms of subscription services in the world is on-demand content delivery. Although it can be used in many industries, the on-demand subscription service model finds application mainly in the media and entertainment sector. You can't talk about this form of subscription without including digital magazines such as the Wall Street Journal and Harvard Business Review. When coming to video-on-demand (VOD), Netflix and Amazon dominate, while audio streaming platforms such as Spotify are popular.

Many of the on-demand content providers charge subscribers a certain fee to access specific content over a given period of time. New and publishing companies typically employ a paywall to allow paid subscribers to access content regular subscribers are restricted from reading or viewing.

With the advent of VOD and online publishing, the days of owning CDs, DVDs, and video games are numbered. Access to streaming movies and music platforms means you can access more content than you could when listening to or viewing content in physical media. In many cases, the amount of content you can access is vast and it can take years to view or listen to all of it. Most importantly, subscriptions to these services cost far less than the cost of buying a CD or DVD. Additionally, many subscription services offer personalization of content, in the manner that social media platforms like X, Facebook, and Pinterest do. A subscriber can receive recommendations of songs, movies, or TV shows based on their subscription platform usage.

VOD

Since VOD is gaining momentum, why not discuss it a bit more? Perhaps this might be the on-demand subscription service model you may like because it's a lot easier to create videos through mobile phone and computer apps. Also, it's a great model if you want to provide online learning in a particular niche such as in raised-bed vegetable gardening.

There are numerous benefits of VOD that make it attractive for subscription services, including the following:

- People prefer to consume content delivered in a video format. It's estimated that the VOD service market will hit $183.93 billion by 2031. Driving factors for this growth include the desire for consumers to receive curated content, increased network speed, and the latest technological advancements. You don't have to go far to prove that video has become a popular format. YouTube, the video sharing platform, is the second-largest search engine behind Google, and ranks second in social media platforms. About 210 million YouTube viewers are from the US.

  A survey study was conducted to understand the importance of video for both marketers and consumers. They found that 73% of consumers would rather watch a short video about a product or service instead of other formats. This was nearly seven times higher than the percentage of people who preferred text-based explanations. Only 3% welcomed a sales call or demo for the same explanation. It's no wonder that 94% of marketers found that video increased consumer understanding of their products or services.

  If this makes you consider using video as the backbone of your on-demand content delivery model, the statistics are in your favor.

- Consumers prefer having a choice and control of what to watch. About 5 million Americans have been canceling their pay-TV subscriptions annually since 2019. Many of these people migrate to streaming services such as Hulu or Netflix. More than three-quarters of Americans, whether they have pay-TV subscriptions or not, have subscribed to streaming platforms. "Cord-cutting," as canceling pay-TV is known, is real, and a huge part of the reason is the user-friendliness of

VOD services. Having options and flexibility is a big requirement of modern consumers.

- Video-focused businesses can create and publish at will. In the past, you had to have a large budget to create video content. After that, you needed methods to influence gatekeepers to access TV network executives. Even then, there was no guarantee that the executive would love your video content. With today's technology, you can present your video content directly to your target audience and do so cheaply.

- VOD is cheaper for the audience than satellite and cable. It can cost more than $200 monthly or $2,400 for a cable subscription. Additionally, you may have to pay extra fees for rental equipment. All these costs are to access content that you may not even like. VOD addresses this problem by providing curated content at bargain prices.

Creating a VOD subscription service business is attractive, especially for niches focused on presenting "how to" content. The process for building this kind of online subscription service business model is the same as for any other type of subscription. The minor tweak to add is creating a library of video content before you begin promoting your business.

The two biggest challenges of on-demand content are consistently providing value your subscribers can't find for free and producing engaging content. If you choose a business idea you like, you will be able to meet both of these drawbacks.

Membership-Based Subscription Service Model

Have you ever browsed a website and when you wanted to access certain content, you got asked to first become a member? If you've ever researched content online for any length of time, you probably encountered this type of scenario. A website created in this fashion is called a membership website. It's nothing but a business built around a membership-based subscription service business model. In this model, a business provides two kinds of content: one for everyone and another for people who pay a recurring fee to access exclusive content or benefits.

It's not only content that gets barricaded, but also opportunities such as access to bargains. For example, you may have an e-commerce membership site that provides members with early access to exclusive products. Can you already see a way to use this model in raised-bed vegetable gardening? One way is to create digital courses and make top-rated ones accessible to paying members. Alternatively, you can create a subscription box and make certain benefits such as discounted prices or free shipping only to paid subscribers. For subscribers to access membership benefits, they'll need to pay the required fee and log in to the platform.

One area that has seen wide application of membership-based subscription survive business models is online learning. During the period of 2011–2021, massive open online courses (MOOCs) skyrocketed their enrollments from 300,000 to 220 million, which is a 732.2 times growth in just 10 years. The good news is that you don't need to be a top online education provider to tap into this market. People became much more interested in non-degree credentials during COVID-19. A non-degree credential is one that helps individuals to improve their professional skills without leading to the acquisition of a degree.

When combining an associate degree with a non-degree credential, 70% believe they're more attractive job hunters. Contrast this with only 43% of those with only an associate degree, and you'll see the value of online education with respect to careers.

Creating a membership-based subscription service business can help you tap into this market and help others reach their career goals as well.

Although this subscription service business model allows for scaling, provides flexibility, and is convenient for members, it can be hard to cater for individual subscribers. Another challenge is that it's not easy to provide personalized learning experiences.

Non-Profit Subscription Service Business Model

Non-profit organizations don't only support various types of charities, but also employ 10% of Americans, which makes up millions of jobs in America. Of these employees, 70% are paid workers. The total income for these types of organizations has increased by more than twice what it was in 2002. What's exciting is that both baby boomers and the younger generations are donating to worthy causes. For example, in 2021, 60% of baby boomers and 57% of Gen Zers donated to non-profit organizations in America. Millennials ranked top on the list of generations that donate the most at an average annual amount of $637, followed by baby boomers at $633, and third was Gen Zers at $553.

If you have interest in operating a non-profit organization, you can start a profitable non-profit subscription service. In a report, it's noted that recurring donors contribute four times more than traditional donors over the life of their donation periods. Best of all, a non-profit subscription service organization can retain up to 95% of its donors, which is about twice that of traditional non-profit organizations.

It can be hard to keep contacting different people to ask for donations. Subscriptions can make it easier for individuals to donate because they're convenient. Your donors won't have to worry about remembering to donate to causes they want to support. This is particularly important because donors prefer to contribute by using credit or debit cards. It's far easier to set up recurring payments made through a credit or debit card than by a check.

Donors care about giving and participating in charities and foundations. However, they don't always enjoy being prompted to make additional donations. This doesn't happen with recurring giving, since donors contribute regularly—usually monthly—making it unnecessary for charities and foundations to prompt them. It feels great for them when they receive fewer solicitation emails and get more communication about how helpful their donations have been.

You can see that you have multiple options when deciding what type of subscription service business to start. All these models help you generate regular income and communicate with your subscribers much more intimately. With this high level of engagement, you can minimize the churn rate and maximize subscriber retention. Before you can learn how to start a subscription service business, let's first find out what mistakes subscription service businesses make.

Checklist

	Determine what type of subscription service business model would be best suited to your industry and niche.
	Decide how you will communicate with your customers and keep them engaged.
	Plan for how you will retain your customers once they are subscribed.

Chapter 3:
Why Some Subscription Service Businesses Fail

Like all types of businesses, subscription service enterprises can fail. Factors that lead to this failure vary from one company to the next. Studying subscription service businesses that failed is a good way to avoid making company-killing mistakes. As much as knowing what to do when building a subscription service business is good, it's as important to know what to avoid. This chapter discusses the elements that trip up subscription service businesses and lead to their failure. If you follow the tips and strategies in this chapter, you can avoid your subscription service business failing within two years—the lifespan of many subscription service businesses.

Let's first look at two stories about failed subscription services before going through five top causes of failure in the subscription service industry.

A Transportation Subscription Service Business That Collapsed

Nick Allen and Rodrigo Prudencio saw a potential gap to provide Uber-like transportation to school children. They founded Shuddle to target parents who wanted a safe mode of transport for their children. Shuddle launched in 2014 but its life was short-lived as it existed for only two years. The reason for its failure was a lack of funds. You're probably wondering how a startup could collapse when backed up by six investors who pumped $12.2 million to the business, right? This query is even more important in that Shuddle had successfully validated its business idea. What happened?

In many families, both parents work or try other means of generating income. Allen and Prudencio recognized that parents, especially mothers, were busy and rarely had time to drive their busy children to school, sports practices, and other after-school activities. Unlike similar companies, Shuddle didn't work as an on-demand service, as parents were required to book the service by at least noon of the previous day. Another differentiator was that Shuddle mostly hired mothers—some of whom were nannies, while others were teachers or coaches. Through its extensive driver-hiring process, Shuddle promised parents that their children would be safe and to deliver children to their respective places in a timely fashion.

Unfortunately, the much-needed service left some of the parents disappointed. Claims arose from online reviews that Shuddle would often cancel bookings in the eleventh hour, which left children and parents in a lurch. Few parents who tried the service rarely renewed their $9 subscriptions. Subscriber retention is central to building a sustainable subscription service business.

On the expenses side, Shuddle didn't do as well as it would have liked. Eventually, Shuddle went back to investors to try and raise funds to stay afloat. This didn't work and the business shut its doors in 2016. Shuddle was unable to raise funds to keep themselves afloat, investing or acquisition opportunities sparse, and they closed down in 2016.

A subscription service must deliver on its promises to its subscribers. When things don't turn out right, it's best to be open and tackle them head-on. Additionally, having money is not a guarantee that your subscription service business will succeed. What you need is the right money, also called cash flow, and ideally from operations. When you start a business from scratch, try to grow it organically and don't compromise on customer service.

A New Orleans Startup Venture That Burned $10.5 Million of Investor Money

Dinner Lab didn't turn a profit during its life and ultimately paid the ultimate price: it failed. The Brian Bordainick-founded startup had raised $10.5 million from venture capital to start the company. With experience in the education sector and project management, Bordainick recruited partners such as Francisco Robert, a former chef at Alinea in Chicago, who understood the food and beverage industry. Despite a wealth of knowledge in cooking and project management, Dinner Lab failed to make money for its investors.

Bordainick conceived the idea of Dinner Lab after noticing that educational entrepreneurs took themselves very seriously. However, he liked the fact that they were willing to experiment and grow. Seeing that this attitude was missing in the culinary space, he decided to form Dinner Lab. Additionally, Dinner Lab aimed at forming communities, an idea Bordainick believes his company achieved.

Dinner Lab offered food and beverage to strangers grouped in one location. To be part of the people who dined at these places, you had to purchase a membership plan and then receive an invitation from Dinner Lab. If things went well, you could participate in 2–5 events that offered this unique experience. The early days didn't go as well as Dinner Lab would have liked. It initially set up dinner events at midnight but quickly found out that members arrived intoxicated. This prompted Dinner Lab to hold events in the early evenings.

Even that didn't help the startup to generate profits. Bordainick's idea of selling memberships and events and using memberships to make a profit didn't work out. Moreover, trying to make profits from selling meals failed to deliver desired results. To keep subscribers happy, it was necessary to innovate regarding meals served, locations, and ingredients used to prepare food. This turned out to be more challenging than initially thought. To make things worse, staff turnover was high.

Notwithstanding these challenges, subscribers enjoyed each dinner experience. Unfortunately, there were fewer events than the company planned. Many subscribers couldn't access some events due to an insufficient number of tickets. If you paid for a membership that promised two events monthly, you'd expect to attend two events a month. But that wasn't always the case at Dinner Lab, as sometimes only one event took place, even if subscribers paid full subscription fees.

Meanwhile, the lack of capital didn't help with increasing the number of events. An attempt to replace full-time employees with contractors to reduce costs didn't help either. The model was too logistically complicated and challenging to become consistent and profitable. Dinner Lab, although a sound business idea, failed in two main areas: complicating the business and failing to deliver what it promised to its subscribers. No business can survive for long if it doesn't provide its patrons with what they've bought. This is especially true with subscription services since subscribers pay upfront to receive a service. Simplicity is key in ensuring that you consistently deliver on what you promise.

Top Five Causes of Failure of Subscription Service Businesses

There are numerous causes of failure to subscription service businesses. Below, we offer five that topple most of these types of businesses.

1. Lack of Novelty

If your subscription business doesn't innovate, subscribers move their dollars elsewhere. Lack of novelty in subscription services is one of the ways that could lead to business failure. Why is novelty so important in subscription service businesses? The answer lies in the way our minds are wired. Before we look at the impact of novelty on the human brain, we should understand what novelty is.

Novelty is about introducing new things in our lives. However, we still need to behave in predictable ways because other business functions depend on this. For instance, you still need to offer predictable customer service for your subscription service to survive. However, that will not move your business to another level.

Suppose that you offer a replenishment coffee subscription box. If all that your subscribers receive are the regular coffee sachets, they lose the excitement they had in the early stages of their subscriptions. They know what they're going to receive, and their curiosity isn't triggered. Because of this, they soon lose interest in their coffee subscriptions. Contrast this with a replenishment coffee subscription box that includes a sample of an unknown coffee and a brochure that tells its origin!

Although subscribers may still grow less interested in the regular coffee brands, they could still keep their subscriptions merely to read the story of the mystery coffee sample you include. Not only could such a story be interesting, but it provides subscribers with new information they can share with friends, family, and colleagues. Doing so makes them feel important, which is a basic human desire that has been critical since the beginning of time. Feeling like we matter is essential because it makes us more confident, raises our self-esteem, and improves our motivation. You can imagine how much your subscribers would love your subscription business if you made them feel worthwhile.

Novelty helps with learning new things so that we can continue to be able to survive in different environments. If your peers are innovating and you're not, your business will become irrelevant over a period of time. This is one of the reasons some subscription service businesses thrive while others just survive—and others still die. Innovate and make yours different by introducing novelty as frequently as is practically possible. Subscription service businesses that innovate will destroy our tendency to get bored quickly.

To win with subscription service businesses, innovate.

2. Lack of Clarity About the Target Subscriber

If we came to you and asked, "Who does your subscription service business target?", what would your answer be? The answer to this question can reveal whether your business has a chance of succeeding or failing. Many subscription service businesses provide vague answers when asked this question. For example, they may say that their target subscriber is a woman who's environmentally conscious. That's fine but it's not granular enough.

How many women who are environmentally conscious are there in the US? If you wanted to send them a marketing message, what media would you use? Are you going to send your message to any woman in the US you believe is environmentally conscious? Theoretically, you can. However, you'll need to have billions of dollars to reach them all, particularly if you want the message to reach them all at once.

Unless you get into detail regarding your target subscriber, your subscription service business has a small chance of survival. Failure to carefully select your target market is one of the quick ways to kill your business.

For instance, let's say you start a cleaning product subscription service. While customers in the United States may be more open to trying a new product or gadget, customers in Italy, may prefer more efficient cleaning products over learning how to use a new tool. It is crucial to conduct market research to ensure that your business is relevant to your intended consumer. Additionally, if you intend to expand your business into other regions, you will need to ensure that your business is adapted to a possibly different audience.

Big companies may be able to absorb financial setbacks. This may not be the case with your subscription service business. Instead, take the time necessary to understand your target subscribers so that you can offer them what they want and can pay for.

3. Excluding Your Mission in Your Offering

Paying low prices is one of the benefits of subscribing to a service. A low price has its place in a subscription service business: to attract bargain hunters. However, it can't help your business retain subscribers. Part of the reason is that people secretly have causes they care about. Many subscription service businesses that fail don't recognize and include their mission in their subscriber offers.

What does a mission have to do with business success? The best way to answer this question is to first understand what a business mission is. A business mission reveals to its employees, customers, and other stakeholders why it exists. Usually, a strong mission should demonstrate that you're ambitious and going after something audacious. A research study was conducted of 49,928 business units in 49 industries from 34 nations to understand if there was any correlation between profit margin and company mission. It was found that these two parameters positively correlate to one another (Groscurth, 2014).

We know that you may create a subscription service to make a lot of money. Can you imagine how customers or subscribers would react if you openly stated that your business exists solely to make money?

You should understand that making money is a result of doing certain things. Specifically, money is a reward you get for serving both your employees and customers. Failure to serve these people will lead your business to the enterprise graveyard. Your mission lets your stakeholders know the driving force behind the creation of your business. A potent business mission is always based on what you value the most. For example, if you value the importance of eating organic foods, you may create a subscription service business that encourages the eating of such foods.

Examples of mission statements are:

- **Universal Health Services, Inc.**: to provide superior quality healthcare services that patients recommend to family and friends, physicians prefer for their patients, purchasers select for their clients, employees are proud of, and investors seek for long-term returns

- **American Express**: become essential to our customers by providing differentiated products and services to help them achieve their aspirations

You'll learn how to define your subscription service business's mission in the next chapter.

4. Inflexible Pricing at the Time of Subscription

Making money is a crucial aspect of any successful startup or business. For subscription businesses, people who subscribe like to have pricing options. Additionally, they want to upgrade or downgrade as they see fit. You'll be excited to know that flexible pricing influences consumers to buy more. Failure to have these options means that subscribers look for alternatives and your subscriber retention declines.

What does inflexible pricing look like? Have you ever visited a subscription-based website only to find that it offers a single price? It's either you buy or don't buy at that price. This kind of pricing strategy doesn't give you options. If you can't afford the price set, it means you can't purchase the service. It'll be disappointing, considering that you wanted the product being sold. Your overall buying experience will be negative.

Contrast that with a subscription service business that offers three pricing options: basic, medium, and deluxe. Each pricing plan will be characterized by certain features that may align with your needs better. Most importantly, you can choose an option that suits you financially. As your needs change, you have options to either upgrade, downgrade, or cancel the subscription. Because of these options, you're likely to have a positive experience with the subscription service.

Do you remember why subscription service businesses are spawning all over the world? Simply because consumers want to have more control when shopping. When your subscription service business doesn't allow for this, subscribers can quickly find another service that does. This should be a concern because such subscribers might influence others far more easily as the world becomes more and more interconnected.

Consumers share their buying experiences online through social media and product reviews. One of the reasons they share these experiences is to warn us, helping potential customers make better buying decisions. Since the pricing of subscriptions is such an important factor, we'll revisit it in the next chapter. Best of all, we will show you how to price your subscription plans.

5. Failure to Involve Subscribers

Imagine that you receive a subscription box at the start of a month. Let's assume that you like the subscription box a lot and you're over the moon the day you receive it. Perhaps the next day you remember the subscription is at the end of the month when you receive your credit card statement and you see the charge. What happens between the day you received the box and the end of the month?

Like most of today's consumers, you'll be inundated with offers of other subscription boxes, streaming services, and other types of subscriptions. The odds of the subscriber renewing are stacked against you. If you recall, churn rates in the subscription industry run anywhere between 4% and 8%. A slight increase in the churn rate could spell trouble for your business. That's possible if you don't consistently stay in the minds of your subscribers.

The way to keep your subscribers hooked is by communicating with them regularly. Communication is especially important in the beginning stages of the subscriber-subscription relationship. The difference between these results is the level of engagement with subscribers during the onboarding process. You can imagine what difference the revenue could be if the churn rate is minimized to a steady 2%.

What if an improved onboarding process was to be combined with other communication methods, such as educating non-converting subscribers over a 30-day period after receiving concierge calls? The best way to find out is to run a test to establish the effectiveness of this strategy. The bottom-line is that you should find ways to engage with subscribers to generate higher conversions.

6. Providing Complex Offers

Giving potential subscribers options at the time they subscribe is great. However, you should avoid making your offers complex because people like simplicity. The same thing applies once a person becomes your subscriber. We're not sure if you've ever tried to search for certain information on YouTube and wound up not knowing which video to watch. Sometimes you try the first few results and if you don't find what you want, you give up.

Fortunately, YouTube can be accessed for free. For YouTube users who have paid subscriptions, it could be frustrating if they don't get the information they want. The next logical thing they're likely to do is unsubscribe and find other options. We understand that YouTube has become a search engine, and this is probably what you're not looking to build.

Instead, try to focus on making your offer as simple as possible. It'll be easy for subscribers to find what they want and use it. That'll add to the value your subscribers are looking for.

Checklist

	Read through the case studies and examples of failed business in this chapter.
	Identify possible challenges you may run into.
	Brainstorm possible fail-safes should any challenges present themselves.
	Determine the longevity and actionability of your business idea.
	Simplify your business idea and minimize the steps needed to make it work.
	Determine how you can offer flexible pricing options.

Chapter 4:

How to Build a Subscription Service Business From Scratch

If you've decided to use a subscription service business model to start your own venture, you need to know how to go about doing so. With this chapter, we provide you with a step-by-step method of building a subscription service business from an idea until you nail your first few subscribers. Since we provide actionable steps, it's a good idea to execute each step as you read this chapter. Do we have a deal? Great, now let's get started with the first key step to take.

1. Find a Subscription Idea for Your Business

As much as a subscription service business is a great model, it's possible to generate a subscription business idea that fails. This means that you should be careful how you generate a business idea, validate it, and scale it. For example, you need to choose an idea that can be scaled so that you can keep increasing your revenue over time. With that out of the way, how do you find a subscription service business idea starting from scratch? Read on to find out.

Write 5–10 things that you like. I'm sure you have a list of things that you like very much. Your list may include items like reading the classics, mountain biking, rock climbing, teaching math, gardening, software development, or playing piano. The more ideas you come up with, the better. Don't try to censor your ideas at this stage. What you want to do is dump all the things you like on a piece of paper.

If you're struggling to generate a list of things you like, how about coming up with a list of 10 things that frustrate you right now? Perhaps you're frustrated by:

- snow shoveling during the winter season

- expensive groceries

- calling customer service

- an endless flow of junk mail

- rush hour commutes

The list is endless. If coming up with a list of at least five items seems like a struggle, hop onto your internet browser and search for things that frustrate a typical American.

Out of the list of what you like, select an idea that you feel you'd be happy to do every day. For example, you may choose the gardening idea if that's what you like the most. It'll be even better if you can narrow the gardening idea down to growing certain vegetables, flowers, or whatever plants interest you. For more possible topics to include, you might sign in on a couple of gardening forums.

Your subscription service business idea might suit using the access subscription model. For example, you might develop software technology or educational content that consumers will need to subscribe to in order to access it. Nothing prevents you from starting a subscription box that provides gardeners with gardening products they need to produce quality vegetables or flowers.

If your idea comes from the frustration list, choose one that you feel you want a solution to as quickly as possible. The good thing about this idea is that you already know what the solution is for your frustration. If you're frustrated about excess junk mail, you could come up with a service for sorting out good mail from junk before the homeowner gets their mail.

These are just ideas to get you started with thinking about a subscription service business you could start. Once you've come up with an idea, you'll need to figure out if it can be turned into a subscription service business. By this, we mean that the service must be recurring and in demand for it to qualify.

2. Research the Market

The aim of market research is to find out if your business idea has an audience that can buy your offer. It follows that your research should reveal who your ideal target audience is, what your competitors are doing to serve them, and what makes your target audience buy from your competitors. Armed with this insider information, you'll be able to find an angle to sell your subscriptions profitably.

The first action to take in your market research is to figure out if there are competing businesses that already offer your kind of product or service. You don't have to look only for subscription-type businesses, but any business that offers what you have in mind. The quickest method to find your competitors is to use search engines like Google or Bing. Let us illustrate how to use a search engine to find and understand your competitors.

We'll assume that you want to start a gardening subscription service business that educates gardeners about growing vegetables using raised beds. Suppose that you want to offer potential subscribers' information such as types of vegetables to grow, their benefits, how to plant them, and many other topics related to vegetables. The easiest subscription service business model to employ would be the access model—mimicking the popular SaaS model.

To find out what your competitors are offering, it's best to search for online blogs that provide content about raised vegetable gardening. Studying a couple of blogs will give you an idea about the type of content the online community wants. Also, check what products these bloggers offer to their audience. In many cases, you'll find that they offer books, courses, and affiliate products.

Two other important sources of competitor information are Udemy and Amazon. The reason we like these marketplaces is that you'll find customer reviews of courses and books, respectively. Not only will you learn about the competition and what frustrates the gardening community, but also what solutions these people want. For example, we searched for vegetable gardening books on Amazon and found one.

The book teaches readers about growing vegetables using raised beds. With more than 5,000 reviews, the topic appears to be of massive interest.

What we like most about these reviews is that you get to learn what pains and frustrations readers want to be solved. For instance, a couple of negative reviews about this book wish that it had included companion planting, more details on how to build a raised bed, and more information on vegetable choices. As you go through the reviews starting from the lowest ratings, you gradually begin to understand what the audience of raised bed vegetable gardening is looking for. It's worth spending a bit of time researching the market because this is the bedrock of your business.

Another source for the frustrations and pains of your audience is forums, in this case, gardening forums. This source is great for finding out what's aching your potential audience.

When done with your research, you should be able to describe them. For example, you might describe them like this: "My subscriber wants to grow vegetables using raised beds. They prefer to know the details of constructing a raised bed, what vegetables to grow together, how to switch vegetables from one season to the next, how to choose the right compost, and how to handle weeds and pests. My gardeners want to produce vegetables that would be the envy of their peers."

You'll notice that we haven't spoken about the demographics of your audience yet. Demographics refers to a set of data about an audience that often includes their age, gender, income, educational background, marital status, and physical address. It is important but not as critical as the pains, fears, and frustrations of your audience—collectively called psychographics. Despite this, demographics are helpful when combined with the psychographics of your audience.

There are several methods for finding the demographics of your target audience, including using SimilarWeb, Semrush, and direct response mailing lists. The good news is that you don't need to subscribe to these tools for this purpose. Let us illustrate how to use Semrush to find the demographics of your potential target audience.

Fire up your browser and go to Semrush.com. On the left pane, select Market Explorer. On the right pane, click on the Find Competitors tab. Where it says, "Enter your domain," type in the domain of your largest competitor (or blog) in the raised vegetable gardening niche. Click on the "Research a market" button. Semrush will return a wealth of data about your online competitors. Scroll down and you'll find a section titled "Domain vs Market: Audience." That's where you can see the age and gender of your target market. To get detailed data, you can subscribe to a free trial to access more data about your potential audience.

Armed with the demographics of your target audience, add them to the description of your target audience created above. You now know who your target audience is and what they want. You also know where they hang out. It's now the time to proceed to the next step of building your subscription service business.

3. Create a Product

Many entrepreneurs fail because they create a product before doing the legwork we've covered so far in this chapter. That's a huge mistake. The reason many such people create products first is that they mistakenly think their target market wants the solution they have in mind. Our approach is different. We know that once we understand our target audience and our competitors, we can create unique and fitting products. Moreover, we'll also have a unique angle to differentiate our business from our competitors.

How do you create a unique product? You have numerous options. You can create software, an app, a blog that includes premium content, video content, a subscription box, or other options. The easiest and perhaps fastest product to create is a subscription website, popularly known as a membership site.

For this website to work well, you'll need to create various types of content. For example, your site may include e-books, video content, audio content, webinars, and perhaps a subscription box. The reason we're suggesting a subscription box is to add it to your premium subscription. Even if your niche is raised-bed vegetable gardening, you can have a package of products that help your subscribers produce delightful and juicy vegetables.

This tells you that the products to create will be the ones I've just mentioned. You don't have to sit at your desk and create each piece of content yourself. There are several ways of getting others to create content for you. For example, you can interview experts in raised-bed vegetable gardening and then turn the content into an e-book and audiobook. Right away, you'll be having three products in one go. What if you repeat this for each topic you know your target audience wants? You could have several products within a month.

If interviewing experts sounds like a hard thing to do, you can hire a freelance writer to write an e-book for you. Then, you can use the e-book as the basis to produce other types of content such as an audiobook or video training. To outsource writing and get a good e-book, you'll need to create a detailed outline. The easiest way we've found to write a good outline is by following a template. A good template should help guide you through the steps of creating an outline. There are numerous free e-book outline templates online to get you started on the right track. Do you get the overall idea of how to create a product?

By the way, a product can also include software. Again, you don't need to be a software developer to produce software. You can simply hire a software developer and work together to create the software you believe will add value to your target audience. In the case of software subscriptions, you can learn a lot from SaaS businesses such as Clickup—a task management system, Duplichecker—a plagiarism software, or Lumen5—a video creation software. The latter has five subscription tiers at the time of this writing.

Once you have two or three products, it's time to think about how you're going to organize and price your subscription service business.

4. Create a Value Proposition

If a potential subscriber asks you, "Why should I subscribe to your service?", what would you say? This question can stump anyone from newbie entrepreneurs to experienced businesspeople. The reason is that very few ever take the time to think about what differentiates their business from their competitors. With the market research you've done coupled with the product geared to benefit your subscribers, you'll be able to precisely answer that question shortly.

To answer that question accurately, you need a unique value proposition. Think about a unique value proposition as a statement that specifically tells your potential subscribers what value they get from your subscription service. When crafted correctly, it tells subscribers why they should opt for your subscription service and not that of your competitors. We might also say that your value proposition differentiates your subscription service from that provided by the competition.

Look at the following examples of value propositions to have an idea about what we're talking about:

1. Unbounce: A/B testing without tech headaches

2. Trello: Trello brings all your tasks, teammates, and tools together

3. Digit: save money without thinking about it

4. Slack: be more productive at work with less effort

5. Shopify: anyone, anywhere, can start a business

It's pretty clear to anyone reading the above value propositions whether you're the target customer or not. If you're the target customer of these businesses, you'll likely find out how it helps you in much more detail.

Before any of the above businesses created their value propositions, they knew what customer pains to solve. They also knew how to position themselves advantageously so that their target audience chooses them.

With that understanding of a value proposition, we now can take you through the process of crafting one for your subscription service business.

1. **Research your target market**. This is the first step that you should have already done at this stage.

2. **Study your competition**. You should also have already completed this step too.

3. **Study your subscription service**. This step helps you identify what your service does for your subscribers. It may have features that make your subscribers happy or relieves them of their pain. Pick out the features that help your subscribers achieve their goals.

4. **Craft your value proposition**. Every potent value proposition has three key elements: headline, subheadline or paragraph, and a visual component such as an image. The headline telegraphs the most important benefit your subscriber will gain for using your subscription service. It should be specific and concise. Check the example value propositions mentioned above to make sense of what we mean by specific and concise. Try to also include the target subscriber in the headline if you can.

   The subheadline elaborates on the headline and includes who your subscription service business serves and why. Adding why it serves a given subscriber helps attract new members to your subscription service.

   Including a visual element simplifies the understanding of your value proposition. You have options such as images, infographics, and video for this purpose. Additionally, a visual element can help grab the attention of your target subscribers.

We know the work above may sound overwhelming. You can make it manageable by getting rid of trying to create a perfect value proposition. Get it done as quickly as you can, and then you can focus on optimizing it as time progresses. The examples of good value propositions you encounter may have undergone multiple iterations to deliver the message intended.

5. Create Subscription Packages and Pricing Strategy

In the beginning, it's not necessary to have a business that offers three tiers of subscriptions. The opportunity to add more tiers will naturally come as you build your business.

It's a good idea to start your subscription business with two plans: the entry plan and the premium plan. The difference between these plans will be the features, content, or products available to the subscriber. You can create tiers to get started with your business. Before you can figure out what your packages should contain, let's first look closely at the different pricing strategies of subscription service businesses.

Subscription Pricing Strategies

One of the most important elements of a subscription service business is pricing. You can't slap any price you want on your subscriptions and get away with it. Your target audience will smell it and take zero action, which is why your prices should align with the industry you operate in. Having said that, your pricing should reflect the kind of services you offer. In short, pricing should achieve three objectives:

- resonate with your target audience

- be in sync with what your brand stands for

- be in line with industry standards

Subscription service businesses often price their services or offers in one of three pricing common strategies: flat rate fee, tiered pricing, and hybrid pricing.

- **Flat-rate pricing**: You can think of this type of pricing strategy as one-tier pricing. The reason is that you offer your subscribers all the features or content on your website or software for a single recurring price. This is typical of membership websites that provide content. We like the fact that the flat-rate fee strategy is simple to implement and easy for your subscribers or potential subscribers to understand. All subscribers pay equal prices and receive the same benefits.

  Flat rate pricing has both pros and cons. Its main advantage is simplicity, making it suitable for a startup. It's also easier to communicate with your target audience, which simplifies selling it. However, one of its major drawbacks is the difficulty in scaling your subscription service business. Potential subscribers might not want some of the features of your offer and feel like they'll be overpaying if they buy the subscription.

- **Tiered pricing**: The second pricing option to consider is called tiered pricing or tiered memberships. Unlike flat fee pricing, this alternative provides subscription options to subscribers. Prices start low but access to features or content is minimal. This changes as you progressively move to higher-priced subscriptions. The most expensive plan boasts a couple of features or content that's excluded in other plans.

  With this pricing approach, potential subscribers have choices that closely reflect their needs and wants. The main benefit of tiered pricing is that you can access a wider target audience, which might be a good way to grow revenue. Some companies that offer tiered memberships usually include an option that appears to be liked by most subscribers.

  Giving potential subscribers too many options could lead to analysis paralysis. This phenomenon is also known as choice overload, and can make it hard for consumers to decide what to buy. Some may end up not buying at all, which isn't good for your business.

- **Hybrid pricing**: This type of pricing approach combines flat rate and tiered pricing. Customers can pay a flat rate for a standard subscription and choose whether they'd like to make once-off payment in between for add-ons they might want.

  The hybrid membership alternative gives members options to personalize their subscription with premium content. It also caters to both short-term and long-term potential subscribers. Communicating this option might not be easy for a startup. You'll need to clearly show value to your potential subscribers and existing members to entice them to spend more.

Now, which of the above pricing strategies do you feel is easier for you to implement? Since your choice isn't cast in stone, you can start with the flat rate option. As you work on your business, you'll adjust your pricing strategies, if need be. There's nothing wrong if you prefer the tiered membership approach right out of the gate. However, the hybrid pricing model is a bit complex for beginners.

How to Set Prices for Your Subscription Service

At this point, you know what pricing model you want to get started with. It's now time to price your subscription. Let's remind you that at this point, you have no business but an idea. Only once you've proven your idea will you have a business. That's why you don't have to be perfect at each stage of building your subscription service business. Here are the steps to follow to set your price:

- **Find out what prices your competitors are charging**. Your business isn't going to operate in a vacuum but rather, in an existing industry. Doesn't it make sense to first find out how many subscribers in your industry are already paying to your competitors? Since it does, search online for competitors already serving your type of subscribers.

Continuing with the gardening example we've used above, we find a lot of competitors who offer subscription boxes. If this is what you want to offer, check the various packages and their pricing. If there are subscriber reviews, read a couple of them to gauge subscriber views on pricing—are they expensive or cheap?

Once you've looked at what competitors are charging for various packages, you'll start having ideas of how to price your service. You'll also figure out what to include in your package for it to stand out from the crowd.

- **Figure out the desired revenue**. The price you choose should allow you to reach your business revenue goal. For a given revenue, a low price means you'll need to have more subscribers than when selling at a high price. For instance, if your monthly revenue target is $5,000 and you sell your subscription at $30 per month per subscriber, you'll need to have 167 subscribers ($5,000/$30 = 166.67). In contrast, if your subscription goes for $40 per month per subscriber, you'll need to have 125 subscribers each month. It's worth trying different combinations of price per subscriber and target revenue until you find a mix that you feel is doable.

Not only should you know how many subscribers you'll need each period but also the cost for serving each subscriber. This is the next element to factor into your subscriber pricing.

- **Estimate the cost of running your subscription service business**. Knowing the revenue you need is fine but not enough. What you want to know is how much money from the revenue will stay in your bank account after all the costs of operating your business—that is, your profit.

To figure out total business costs, estimate how much it costs for supplies, website hosting services, shipping and handling, subscriber acquisition costs, and any other business expense. When you have that total, subtract it from your total revenue to work out the profit. For instance, if the total monthly costs are $3,000 and the revenue is $5,000, then your profit is $2,000 ($5,000 - $3,000 = $2,000) each month.

As I mentioned earlier, start with one or two subscription packages to jumpstart your business. As the business grows and you get to understand your subscribers better, you'll create more packages to cater to their different needs and preferences.

At this point in your journey to building a subscription service business, you have found a business idea, researched your market, created products, and priced your subscription. Gradually, you're nearing the time to validate your idea. But first, you need tools to run your subscription service.

6. Choose the Minimum Technology You Need for Your Business

Operating a successful subscription service business requires having a well-oiled system. This system has to carry out various functions, including marketing, handling customer relationships, capturing website data, and handling recurring payments. We wish there was a single technology that could perform all these functions but there are none so far. This means you have to select the individual parts and connect them to create a working system.

Fortunately, many have already done the hard work and we know what technology to have for your subscription service business. What's challenging is selecting the right technology from the ever-increasing number of them on the market. Once you know what type of technology you need, the selection process becomes much easier. Here are the minimum technologies you'll need for an online subscription service business:

Website: Your Main Workhorse

The first technology you need is a functioning website. All the other technologies will rely heavily on the quality of your website. The good news is that you can build your own website without the need to learn how to code. What's most important is knowing the purpose of creating your website. In this case, you know you want a website for running a subscription service business.

Other elements that go into building a website include choosing the right domain name and a hosting service. Your domain should be memorable and relate to the type of audience you want as subscribers. For instance, if you're in the raised-bed vegetable gardening niche, you may choose a domain name such as organicraisedbedgardening.com. As for hosting, it's a great idea to use a service provider that provides reliability and high availability for your website.

Another important part of having a functioning website is choosing an appropriate website builder. There are many free website builders, depending on the type of content management system (CMS)—discussed below—that you can use.

When designing and building your website, ensure that it speaks to your audience in terms of its elements, such as structure and images. The research you completed on your competitors will come in handy when designing your website.

Of course, even if you outsource the building of your website, you still need to know what you want. A web designer will build you a website that meets your needs.

CMS

Your website alone isn't going to do what you want unless you have a CMS and other tools. A CMS allows you to create content on your website without having hard-to-learn technical knowledge. This means that you don't need to know how to write code, and many times, there's no need to understand it at all.

To create content, you won't have to learn and understand HyperText Markup Language (HTML) and how to upload it to your server. All it takes is typing up your content the same way you would on Microsoft Word.

There are many CMS applications such as WordPress, Joomla, Wix, and Drupal. WordPress is the most popular of these, with a market share of 65.1%. When choosing a CMS, consider ease of use, scalability, and security. Don't forget to choose a CMS that's compatible with the other technology you need for running your subscription service business.

Website Analytics

How do you improve a business whose metrics aren't measured? Where do you even start with your improvement initiatives in such a business? It's hard to improve a business if you don't measure its key performance metrics. To improve any given business metric, you first have to know where it currently stands. This is where website analytics come into play for any online business, such as many subscription service businesses.

A website analytics tool provides you with the data you need to understand your online business. For instance, you can identify what type of content resonates with visitors, where your website visitors come from, and how effective your customer service is to your subscribers.

Website analytics tools come in many variations, from simple to complex, and pricing. You can get Google Analytics, one of the most powerful website tools, for free. Google doesn't mind handing you this tool for free because you feed it with valuable data. Other free similar tools include Hotjar, Open Web Analytics, and Clicky. Paid website analytics tools such as Adobe Analytics can be expensive for a startup. It's far more cost-effective to start with a free tool and upgrade when you need a paid version for accessing better data.

The most important function of website analytics tools is to measure user behavior on your website. When you understand what attracts users, you can devise a plan to keep drawing them to your website. Best of all, you'll also know what makes them become your subscribers.

The key when approaching website analytics tools is selecting one that meets your needs and can measure the metrics you want.

Recurring Billing System

Another crucial technology you need is a recurring billing system. A billing system can be manual or automatic. We prefer an automatic version because it relies little on human involvement. This type of system automates activities such as payments, invoicing, and document preparation. As such, it also provides additional insights to successfully run your subscription service business.

Having a recurring billing system is a win-win for both you and your subscriber. It helps avoid doing the repetitive manual task of invoicing your subscribers each period. Because of its automation, it can help keep subscribers for longer than if the setup were manual, which bodes well for your revenue. The subscriber doesn't have to worry about ensuring they pay for their subscription. This means they keep the subscription alive and keep receiving the benefits until they cancel.

Marketing and Marketing Automation

Marketing is a crucial element for the success of any business. Why is that? Marketing allows you to climb into the mind of your customer. It lets you understand your customers so that you can fit your product and service to them. The aim is to let your product or service sell itself.

This wasn't easy in the era of pens, paper, and calculators. Direct response copywriters had to send marketing material to their prospects and customers by mail. Then, they had to collect responses and other customer data manually. As you can imagine, it was a laborious and time-consuming process. Today, we can use specific technology to collect similar data and more.

The purpose of collecting information about customers and prospects was to understand them deeply. In that way, marketers know that it becomes much easier to sell your products and services. Before we delve into marketing automation, why not first understand what marketing is? Marketing is everything that a business does to attract and retain customers or subscribers. In this way, the business can sell more of its products and services. When you perform the marketing function well, selling becomes easier.

At the heart of marketing is market and consumer research so that you can produce and present desired content. The content produced is so valuable that the potential customer or subscriber feels compelled to want to do business with you. That's why marketing infiltrates nearly all parts of a business, whether product development or advertising. There can't be effective product development without market research, which is a function of marketing.

Some of the tasks of marketing are repetitive and can be automated. For example, you can automate the sending of content to your subscribers through emails. This is where marketing automation software like AWeber, Mailchimp, and Infusionsoft come into play. Some customer relationship management (CRM) software can also be used for this purpose. Automating your marketing efforts frees you up to focus on tasks you absolutely must do, such as market research.

One of the powerful features of most marketing automation technology is collecting customer behavior data. For instance, it can measure email open rates, which is helpful to establish what kind of headlines resonate with your target audience. Using this technology, you can automate content delivery at all stages of the marketing process, including awareness, consideration, and conversion.

Some of the marketing automation technology is available for free for the basic version. This allows you to start using them without having to fork out cash upfront. As your business grows, you can use the cash generated to purchase premium plans and access better features.

Order Management System

The quickest way to kill your business is to fail to fulfill your subscribers' orders quickly. You can imagine how frustrating it is when your subscriber anticipates receiving their subscription box but doesn't get it! Some people abscond work on the day they expect to receive certain packages. If such people don't get their packages, they're within their rights not only to be frustrated but to unsubscribe from your service.

Your subscription service business can avoid this kind of situation by using an order management system (OMS). This is useful for both online and offline subscriptions. For online subscriptions such as content products and software, subscribers can access them at any time. All the subscriber has to do is log in to access them. An OMS is much more important for subscription businesses that provide physical products such as subscription boxes.

There are at least four functions that the OMS you choose must accomplish: order placement, order fulfillment, inventory management, and after-sales service. As soon as someone becomes a subscriber, the OMS must kick in to ensure that the new subscriber receives their order in a timely manner. Additionally, this system must keep doing this as long as the subscriber hasn't canceled their subscription.

Inventory management is crucial to ensure that no subscriber waits too long to receive their products. This means that the OMS must synchronize with supplier systems to ensure there's always inventory for subscribers. In the event where there's no inventory, there must be a method for ensuring the subscriber still receives their products quickly.

When choosing an OMS, remember each of its steps presents an opportunity to provide excellent customer service. Ensure that the system you choose allows you to build this important business function in it.

Customer Relationship Management

Email marketing software is great for running marketing campaigns. As your number of subscribers grows, you'll have many people to interact with. This can make it hard to keep track of each customer and their actions. This is where customer relationship management (CRM) tools come in handy.

A CRM simplifies the storage of data about subscribers and potential subscribers and helps you understand subscriber behaviors. Moreover, it makes it easy to track any communication between subscribers and your business. Without a tool like this, information about your subscribers will be scattered all over social media, email marketing software, and your business's website. This will make it difficult to build a coherent picture of each of your subscribers.

By employing a CRM, you can consolidate all the data about every one of your subscribers. The good news is that modern CRM technologies can combine contact management, chatting, and marketing automation. However, if you already have a marketing automation tool, it's better to choose an analytics CRM instead of an operational version. An analytics CRM focuses on data collected from various sources for analysis while the operational type performs similar functions to marketing automation tools. Some of the analytics CRM tools you may want to explore include Alteryx, Hubspot, and Creatio.

Payment Recovery Solution

It's easy to assume that every subscriber will pay to renew their subscription. Reality suggests a different picture. People forget, and this could happen to your subscribers. For example, they may pay for other services and products and remain penniless on their credit cards or in their checking accounts. When your billing system charges them, the transactions may be declined. This will obviously negatively impact your revenue.

Something else that you might not realize is that your subscriber retention may also decline. As stated earlier, if this happens, your expenses will increase. Consequently, your profit will also decrease, which isn't good. How can you ensure that declined charges are at a minimum? The solution is to use a payment recovery solution, which is also called dunning software or simply dunning.

How this solution works is that when your billing system records a declined charge, the dunning software notifies the subscriber about the failure. This is like a call center agent calling to inform you that you've missed making an installment payment, such as on that of a car. Doing this is another strategy for providing customer service, which helps decrease subscriber churn.

One of the challenges with sending emails is that they could end up in the spam folder. You need to choose a dunning software that integrates with marketing automation and CRM tools.

7. Craft a Sales Page for Your Subscription Offer

The purpose of a sales page is to persuade potential subscribers to become actual subscribers. It's a special landing page in which you describe your offer in full. Many people struggle to craft a sales page that gets the job done, which is why we're including a guide to help you write an impactful one. Your success in creating a subscription service will hinge largely on how well you convert visitors into subscribers.

Two Versions of Sales Pages

Sales pages come in two general forms; long-form and short-form. A short-form sales page typically sells products or services in which readers need little convincing. In many cases, the prices of the products or services being sold are low. For example, if you had to sell a loaf of bread online, you'll simply describe a few of its features and benefits and ask the reader to buy it.

Most e-commerce sales pages that you encounter are examples of short-form sales pages. This makes sense, since readers don't want to spend a ton of time reading about a battery or similar product before making a buying decision.

A long-form sales letter can be a couple of thousand words in length. They generally take a bit of time to read and complete. The reason is that long-form sales letters provide in-depth information about the subscription service. You don't write a long-form sales page for the sake of it; you do so because potential subscribers need detailed information and reasons why they should buy the product or service. Most importantly, long sales pages have to convince the reader to part with their money.

The Main Components of a Sales Page

Sales pages that convert visitors into customers or subscribers contain the same elements. If yours include these elements in the right order, you could sell numerous subscriptions the day you launch it. These common elements include the headline, subheadline, subscription service description, testimonials, offer description, call-to-action, urgency, and guarantee. We describe each of these elements in the order they generally appear on a sales page below:

- **A powerful headline**: The first element that readers of a sales page see is the headline. It's usually the power of the headline that makes readers want to read the rest of the sales page. Unless you make it strong, you'll lose many potential subscribers. A strong headline usually includes a benefit to the reader, a news element, and curiosity. If you offer a chocolate subscription box at a huge discount, you could write a headline like this: "How a lover of chocolate scored a 55% discount on her Swiss-made chocolates."

- **Subheadline**: The subheadline expands or gives more details about the headline. A subheadline suitable to work with the headline above could be: "Discover how Jane accidentally found a chocolate subscription box that has never been revealed to the public before, until now."

- **Introduction**: This is a good place to show that you understand the pain point of your subscribers. For example, if you sell a vegetable subscription, you could say "If you're tired of buying vegetables every week, this page provides you with a way out." Alternatively, you could open your sales page with the relevant story.

- **Benefits**: Once you've introduced your solution to a pain point, it's time to provide more details about the pain point and the solution you offer. It's a good idea to describe the benefits the reader will gain by using your solution. This is where you can also mention the features of your solution and how they benefit the subscriber.

- **Testimonials**: For social proof, add testimonials or academic research to back up your claims of benefits. Testimonials are better because they add social proof to your sales efforts.

- **Answer objections you expect from the reader**: Readers often object to what they hear. For example, they may ask, "How do you know this solution will work for me?" Your job is to provide an explanation for questions such as these, although they may not be expressed. Many times, you may do this throughout your sales message by including a reason for making certain claims. You can also do this part by having a short frequently asked questions (FAQs) section.

- **Offer**: Describe your offer and pricing. Also, provide a reason for pricing your offer the way you have. If you have bonuses to add, indicate the value of each. In the case where you offer a discount, clearly explain why you're doing so because people are skeptical.

- **Add a CTA**: Tell the reader exactly what to do to buy. Explain what will happen after the reader has clicked on the CTA. To add urgency, include a timer to encourage faster decision-making.

The above elements will help a great deal when crafting a sales page. Include all of them so that your sales page converts at a rate that's profitable.

8. Validate Your Subscription Service Business Idea

You've worked over the past few weeks to find a subscription business idea, researched the market, decided on pricing, and found the technology you need (most of these can be for free or be available on a free trial basis). You're now ready to test your business idea.

How you test the idea will depend on whether you're doing it online or offline. Offline approaches include sending snail mail or meeting potential subscribers in person to pitch your idea. Using snail mail allows you to target the type of audience that matches the people you want as subscribers. There are targeted mailing lists you can mail to. The challenge with direct mail is that it can be expensive and time-consuming to create and get feedback. Meeting the right type of people you want is hard. How do you even know that a person you meet on the street matches your target audience?

We suggest using online methods because they tend to be cheaper and faster. This means you can test a couple of ideas quickly and have a better chance of hitting a jackpot. In this section, we'll explain how to validate your idea using this approach.

We assume that you already have a website, a marketing automation tool, a recurring billing system, and an OMS. If you don't have them yet, give yourself a couple of hours and search for them online and choose what you feel will be the right fit. When done, take the following steps to validate your idea:

- **Create a lead magnet**. A lead magnet is a product that you offer potential subscribers in exchange for their contact details, such as a name and email address. A lead magnet comes in many formats, including a whitepaper, report, video, email course, or e-book. The easiest lead magnet to offer is content in the form of a report or short e-book.

Even if your business idea is a subscription box, you can create information related to it as a lead magnet. If you can't write but can speak, create an audio recording using your phone or computer. Give your lead magnet an enticing title similar to what you see in many successful books. If you're in raised-bed vegetable gardening, you can use titles such as "How we skyrocketed the yield of our raised-bed vegetable garden by 88%."

- **Create a landing page**. This is a website page meant to achieve only one objective. In this case, your objective is to collect the contact details—name and email address—of potential subscribers. Some of the marketing automation tools have landing page templates that you could populate with your own information. You don't need to have a perfect landing page. All you need is a headline (like a news headline in a magazine or newspaper), a description of what you're offering and its benefits to the user, and a call-to-action (CTA). We suggest that you offer information.

When a potential subscriber enters their name and email, your marketing automation tool will add them to an email list.

- **Craft a series of nurturing emails**. If you ran an offline store and a potential customer came in, what would be the first thing that you'd do? Greet and welcome them, right? Why would you approach your online potential subscribers differently? You treat them exactly the same as if they had visited your physical store but by using emails. One advantage of using emails is that you can create multiple email touchpoints—called an email sequence—with your email list before asking them to buy what you offer.

There are various types of email sequences, including nurturing email sequences. This is the type that you use to deliver your lead magnet and welcome the email subscriber to your email list. Include the benefits the email subscriber will gain for being part of your email list. It's also here where you can ask your email subscriber to whitelist your email address so that your email doesn't end up in their junk mail, that is, their spam box. Most importantly, end the email with a statement that informs the reader that they'll receive a second email in the next two days. Tease them about what the email will be about and how it'll benefit them.

The second email of the series should begin to build a relationship with your potential subscribers. How do you do this? You can approach this in many different ways. One of the best methods is to introduce your business and why you created it. This is where it would be clear that you've created your enterprise to serve them. Again, tease the email subscriber about what the next email will be about in the next two days.

Your third email provides content that adds value to your email list. Obviously, you're not going to cover the content in detail. It's also in this email that you let your email subscribers know that you have a product that could help them to solve their problems. Inform them that you'll give them more details in the next email.

The fourth email delivers on the promise you made in your third email. Describe your product or service by using words that clearly show how your email subscribers will benefit. Use this email to also make an offer to your email subscribers. You'll learn more about how to make an offer later in the book. The most important element of an offer is making it irresistible by including discounts, guarantees, and bonuses for paid subscriptions. You can also offer a free trial if it suits your business.

In the next three emails, you focus on making follow-ups to try to get as many email subscribers to buy your product or service as possible.

All these emails must be set up before going to the next step. It's important to test if the setup works as planned. A good marketing automation software should allow you to run these tests. You don't want to face issues when you go live with your email sequence.

- **Send traffic to your landing page**. With your email sequence set up, you're ready to send traffic to your landing page. Traffic means people who visit your website. The fastest method of finding and sending traffic to your landing page is using pay-per-click (PPC) advertising. This means that you pay only when someone clicks on a link or button you want them to click.

  You can use Facebook ads, Instagram ads, X ads, Pinterest ads, or Google Ads, depending on where your target audience congregates the most. All these sources simplify the placement of ads on their platform. Make sure that you limit the advertising budget to avoid spending more money than you actually have.

If all goes well, you should start making money in four to seven days from the first day you run traffic to your landing page. Typically, if you get a couple of email subscribers, it's a sign that there are people interested in your business idea. However, it's only when they buy that you'd have truly validated your idea.

What if no one buys? Try another business idea. The good news is that this time you'll be quicker because you would have already gained experience when exploring your first idea.

If someone buys your subscription, then you need to take steps to keep them interested.

9. Onboard Your New Subscribers Seamlessly

When is the first time that you get in contact with a potential subscriber? For some subscription businesses, it's when they meet people in person during market research. If you do your market research online, the first time a potential subscriber engages with your business might be when they subscribe to your email list. Whether you first meet your potential subscriber offline or online, the event represents an onboarding experience. The reason is that the potential subscriber immediately gauges if they'd like to be a part of your business or not.

It follows that the nurturing email sequence described above is crucial for your seamless onboarding experience. Even if you meet people offline or via snail mail, how you make them feel influences their decisions about being a part of your business. That's why it's essential to make sure you put your best foot forward when first interacting with them.

Once a person becomes your new subscriber for your subscription service, you also need to take the relationship to a higher level. This is where a formal onboarding process to a subscription becomes critical. Onboarding is nothing but the way you initiate a new subscriber to your subscription service or product. Its aim is to make a new subscriber feel like they've come to the right place.

One of the crucial reasons for effective onboarding is that it begins your subscriber retention efforts. When you bring in new subscribers, you don't know them as well as you could because you have limited information about them. If they stay with you longer due to your effective onboarding process, you can collect as much information about them as possible. Having this information allows you to add the kind of value your subscribers hope for. Subscriber retention means you'll achieve an improved LTV. Potentially, since your subscribers will be happy, they'll likely refer their family, friends, or colleagues to try your subscription service. Doing onboarding wrong is shooting yourself in the foot and your subscription service business won't thrive: At best, it'll just survive while its peers are flourishing.

How do you execute a flawless and effective onboarding experience for your new subscribers? We'll illustrate this process, assuming you run an online subscription service business. Here's what to do:

- **Send a welcome email**. The first step to take is to send your new subscriber a welcome email. Thank them for purchasing the subscription option they prefer and let them know how enthusiastic you are that they've joined your business. Tell them that you're even more thrilled to help them nail their goals. Most importantly, reiterate the benefits they'll get for the subscription choice that they've opted for. This is also a great time to provide the subscriber with their login details.

- **Greet them with a message after they've logged on.** This message is different from the welcome email described above. Its purpose is to inform the subscriber about the next steps they should take. Many subscriptions require new subscribers to set up their account. Your new subscriber doesn't know how to do this on your platform. They therefore need to be guided on doing this. It's far more effective and simpler for the new subscriber to follow a video guide than a text guide. For this reason, we suggest creating a short video guide to achieve this purpose. Also, include steps to change a password and email preferences.

- **Guide them about the product or subscription setup.** The next step is to create a video tutorial to explain how the product or subscription they've chosen works. It's advisable to make this guide as short as possible. Since products and subscriptions vary, you might not need this step, or you can make it optional.

- **Explain each feature of your subscription.** This is particularly important where there are features that have no data. Try not to leave them empty; instead, fill them with content, educational or action-focused, to add value to your subscribers.

- **Add frequently asked questions (FAQs) in the subscriber portal.** We understand that this may be hard in the beginning. However, you can find out what common FAQs the market often asks from search engines such as Google. This search engine has a section called "people also ask" on its search results page. These questions can be a good start. Additionally, you can check what FAQs your competitors have included on their websites and use them as inspiration in creating yours and their answers.

- **Send check-in emails**. Once or twice a week, send emails to check in with your subscribers. You may also use these emails to direct them toward certain resources on your subscription platform. Doing this shows your subscribers that you care and can tip the scales in your favor and help improve the customer LTV of your business.

To reiterate, your business will struggle unless you onboard your new subscribers effectively. Building a business is like completing a puzzle, except that you need to follow a sequence of steps. This chapter has provided you with the steps you need to get your subscription business idea off the ground. By following them, you'll greatly improve your chances of building a thriving subscription service business.

You may be wondering how to go about building a subscription service business if converting from a traditional business. That's a great undertaking, and we tackle it in the next chapter.

Checklist

	List 5-10 problems you'd like to solve or ideas you have for a subscription service.
	Conduct market research to ensure you reach your intended customers.
	Determine whether you will create or source products and start the process.
	Create a value proposition to organize your business and make its intention clear.
	Plan your packages and pricing strategy.
	Choose the technology you need to run your business.

	Draft your sales page.
	Create a lead magnet and set up your landing page.
	Plan and draft your retention emails.
	Tailor your onboarding process and start welcoming new customers.

Chapter 5:
How to Convert to a Subscription Business Model From a Product or Service

The benefits of subscription services are enticing. Converting or introducing subscription services to your business could boost your revenue. Most importantly, it could enhance the relationships you have with your subscribers and customers and improve the profitability of your business. However, converting to a subscription service requires completely rethinking your customers. You would also need to use tools that you've never used before. Fortunately, we provide a guide on how to navigate the challenges you may face.

Why Do You Want to Convert to a Subscription Business Model?

The biggest attraction to subscription services is recurring revenue and profitability. But you have to do quite a bit of legwork to convert to a subscription service from a product or service. As a result, you need to think through your reasons for converting. We're talking about specific reasons that apply to your business, and not general ones like the fact that you'll receive recurring revenue.

One example of companies that successfully converted from physical products to subscription services is Adobe, the creative software company. In an interview with McKinsey, Mark Garrett, then the company's chief financial officer, revealed the forces that compelled Adobe to make the transition. Among those drivers, the company was struggling financially and also needed to make the change due to strategic reasons. For instance, the company couldn't keep up with the pace of innovations its customers required, and technology advanced at a faster rate. Trying to produce physical products at those rates was undoable. Additionally, Adobe faced financial struggles due to the 2008–2009 financial meltdown, and this contributed to the decline of its stock price. Its customers were also happy with the products that they purchased, which meant there was no reason for them to buy anything else from the company. As a result, the company had to keep looking for new customers. The solution that the company settled on, after doing extensive research, was to migrate to subscription services.

As you can see, Adobe was clear about why it needed to switch to subscription services. You should do the same. The starting point is understanding your current business model and evaluating whether transitioning to subscription services is the right move or not. Think about how much work needs to be done to make the shift: mindset changes, creating suitable subscription products, appropriate marketing plans, and subscriber-retention strategies. You wouldn't want to make a fast shift only to discover later that the move wasn't warranted. That's why what we're about to explain and discuss next is so crucial.

How to Evaluate Your Current Business Model

To transition to the subscription service business model, you first have to evaluate your current model. The results of your evaluation will guide you on what precisely you can shift to subscriptions and what to keep as is. The work you do during this phase of your transition will guide the rest of the tasks still to be done.

Evaluating your current business model means you'll need to take a close look at all the business aspects such as customers, marketing, business culture, products or services you sell, operations, and customer retention strategies. You also need to assess the strengths and weaknesses of your existing business model. The items we describe below provide a good approach to evaluating your business:

- **Who are your current customers?** Every business exists for one reason only: to provide a desired product or service to a specific group of customers. You may have started your business being unclear about who your target market is. Alternatively, you may have known your target audience, but the reality might have turned out differently. Irrespective of what you may have thought about your customers when you started, you can't guess who you currently serve. Your customers pay for everything in your business and therefore, they're the real bosses. So, who is your real boss? You should have collected data from various sources to know who your customers are. If you don't already have this information, we'll guide you on what to do shortly.

- **What products or services are your customers buying?** There should be no doubt about what products or services your customers are purchasing. The proper running of any business includes maintaining a regular stock of all products, which necessitates knowing which products customers buy in large numbers. The same can be said about services. You should have no doubt how many customers buy your service each month.

- **What value are your customers getting?** This question is about why customers buy from you. It can be hard to figure this one out by yourself. This is where things like testimonials and online reviews can come in handy. Additionally, you may run surveys where you ask your customers questions that will help you understand why customers buy your products or services. Get as much information as possible. If you have salespeople, ask them a lot of questions about customers and why they buy certain products or services.

- **How are you currently promoting your brand, products, or services?** No matter how good or how much your customers love your products or services, you'll need to promote them. The reason is that there are potential customers who just need to be nudged a bit to buy. It's your job to do the nudging, which is where promoting your products, services, or brands comes in. Are you promoting your products or services through a blog, direct mail, word-of-mouth, PPC advertising, or through seminars and other live events? Finding out what channels work best in generating sales not only will help when you promote subscription services, but also shed light on what works currently. As a result, you can decide to spend money only on channels that make you better ROI.

- **How are you distributing your products or services?** When you run a business that sells low-margin products, especially an online retail business, you need to sell a lot of them to make a reasonable amount of profit. This requires you to ship all products bought by your customers, which is where you need transportation. Alternatively, you may be distributing your products through retail establishments. If selling services, you may be getting them to your customers through the internet or sending employees to your customers' homes. There should be no guess as to what your channels of distribution are.

- **What tasks do you perform to provide value to your customers?** Each business function ultimately contributes to the value that your customer receives. The simplest approach to figuring this out is by following the functions that need to be performed from product or service idea right through to customer service or support.

- **How is your business performing financially?** The ultimate test of how well your business functions is its finances. Check for metrics such as revenue, gross profit, operating profit, net income, and cash flow. Are they increasing from year to year, stagnant, or declining? Declining revenue or operating profit is a sign that something fundamental is wrong within your business.

- **Is your business scalable?** Some businesses are easy to expand while others take too much effort. It's highly possible to scale a subscription service business or an online business without increasing expenses. Such isn't the case for most traditional businesses. How's yours going to scale as time progresses?

- **Are there opportunities to introduce subscription services?** Since you already know what subscription services are, you might spot opportunities to adopt them as you evaluate your business. For example, if you have products or services that customers want regularly, you could turn them into subscriptions. However, if you don't have such products or services, you'll need to create them from scratch or consider creating a curation subscription service. What's crucial at this stage is understanding if subscriptions could be of value or not. When you realize that subscriptions can make your business and customers better, it's time to take other transitioning steps.

Research and Understand Your Current Customers

Unlike a startup, an existing business already has customers. However, this doesn't mean that you should simply switch from a traditional to a subscription service business. What if your existing customers have no affinity for a subscription service? All your time and effort to convert to a subscription service would have gone to waste.

It's far better to approach the conversion to a subscription service as if you're starting from scratch. The main difference between a typical startup and your conversion is the fact that you have a wealth of information about your customers and competitors. Doing customer and competitor research should be simpler. We'll first begin by doing customer research to establish what kind of subscription service is suitable.

Figure Out What Your Customers Want

The purpose of finding out what your customer wants is to create the right subscription service at the right price. It's far easier to sell something to someone if you know what they want and why they want it.

We assume that by this time, you already have the demographics and psychographics of your existing customers. However, you still need to confirm if these are still true and avoid making costly assumptions. You can quickly locate this information by analyzing your analytics.

Once you've verified the demographics and psychographics of your customers, it's time to find out what they think about your subscription idea. What are the things that you're going to figure out about your customers? This is one of the reasons you had to evaluate your current business model. You should have realized that you could convert one or more of your products or services to subscription services.

For example, if you retailed milk to your neighborhood, you may have found that you could deliver it to your customers' doorsteps. Perhaps further research showed that you could deliver the milk every Monday and still make money. There's more you'll still need to do.

You can conduct customer interviews or run surveys to strengthen the results of your research. If you run an online business or have email addresses of your customers, it's easier to run an email survey. The aim of these interviews and surveys is to establish if your customers would be interested in a subscription service idea you have. As a result, you should ask questions such as the following:

- How often do you use our product or service? Do you use it once daily, weekly, monthly, or annually?

- What do you like most about our product or service?

- What do you dislike most about our product or service?

- Would you still like our product or service if we increased its price?

- Would you still like our product or service if we decrease its price?

- If we offered you a subscription service to receive the same product or service for a discounted fee, would you like it?

- What else would you like to get with your subscription?

- How much would you be willing to pay for the subscription?

The above questions should get your mind foraging for better questions related to your existing business. Use them as guides to the creation of survey or interview questions pertaining to your product or service.

At the end of your customer research, you should have a subscription service idea that you can later validate. Don't be surprised if you may have to offer a completely new product or service. If your customers want it, it's your duty to provide it if you want to stay in business.

What's the Competition Doing?

Business success requires studying not only your customers, but also your competitors. This allows you to notice changes in your industry and keep pace with them. We're reminded about a 2015 interview that McKinsey held with Adobe, the cloud software company. At that time, Adobe was sharing how it transitioned to a cloud company from a business that delivered shrink-wrapped creative suite software.

When asked why Adobe made that transition, the then vice president of business operations and strategy, Dan Cohen reasoned as follows:

> When we looked at how other software companies were faring during the recession [2008-2009], we saw that companies with high recurring revenue had smaller declines in their growth rates and valuations. We had a very big drop in both—our revenue dropped about 20 percent, and our valuation fell even more."

We can see clearly that Adobe had to research its competitors before making a transition to a subscription service model. Most importantly, it was lagging behind its peers, both financially and strategically.

Like Adobe, you need to evaluate the competition in your industry. Ask yourself what they're doing. Are there new subscription service businesses that have sprung up? What are businesses that are operating the transactional business model doing about it? Most importantly, is there a market for new subscription service businesses in your industry? The answers to the above questions will provide insight into the state of your industry.

What if you discover that there's no competitor who's running a subscription service model in your industry? In that case, ask yourself why that is the case. Have there been other businesses that have tried the recurring model and failed? Have any businesses not tried this exciting business model? Asking these questions will trigger you into digging deeper and finding out if a subscription service model can work in your industry.

Create a Value Proposition

Now that you've evaluated your existing business model and researched your customers and the competition, you can proceed to creating a compelling value proposition. Subscribers want to know what you offer them, and you also want to stand apart from your competitors. That's what your value proposition will do.

We have gone through the process of creating a value proposition in Chapter 4. The process will be the same as when creating a subscription service business from scratch.

Unlike when starting from scratch, you'll probably have two value propositions: one for the traditional business and another for subscriptions. The reason for this is that we recommend you convert one product or service at a time into a subscription. This means that you'll add subscriptions to what you already have.

Establishing Your Pricing Strategy

The pricing strategies we discussed in Chapter 4 apply equally to converting to a recurring revenue business model. You need to decide upfront which pricing will help you achieve your goals. We'd like to make additional points to bear in mind when choosing your pricing strategy.

At the start of a subscription service business model, cash flow can be tight. The reason for this is that subscription acquisition costs may be high relative to the price of your subscription. As a result, it'll take a bit of time to break even. Don't make the mistake of choosing a pricing strategy that'll be too hard on your business to break even, though. Remember that having cash is far more important and too low a price could put a strain on it.

A good example of a pricing strategy is to offer discounts instead of offering your services or goods for free in the first month. You can offer a discount in the first two or three months to a potential subscriber who buys a six-month subscription. Your research into your customers will ultimately provide the best guide on your pricing strategy. Warning: Subscribers may not know for sure what price is right for them. That's why you should run price tests until you find one that works for both you and your subscribers.

Select the Right Technology

Your subscription service will need special technology for it to work. We've described the minimum technology needed in the previous chapter. Head over there to remind yourself what technology is needed.

Test Your Subscription Service

Your first subscribers will be your existing customers: they'll be shifting their mode of buying from one-off purchases to recurring buying. We indicated earlier that you may be served well by segmenting your customers. If you've done this, you'll find it easier to test your subscriptions to one of the segments.

Choose a certain customer segment and test your subscription service idea on it. Then, you can follow the same process of validating your subscription service the same way as described in Chapter 4. The difference is that your first email will be the third in the nurturing email series explained in Chapter 4. In this email, you introduce your new subscription service.

The most important realization is that you need to adapt your selling approach. It's no longer about selling your products or services but about selling subscriber experiences. Your subscriptions are meant to make life easier for your subscribers.

Those who buy should also receive subscriber support emails through your onboarding process as described in Chapter 4. Your intention is to get them to renew at the end of their subscriptions, and this is where Chapter 7 will come in.

Now, if your launch is successful—you define this yourself—you can extend the offer to customers in other segments. It may happen that things don't go as you plan. That's fine; that happens to the best minds in business. Analyze your data to find out where the problem lies and make corrections.

Checklist

	Determine what services and products your customers are buying.
	Determine a plan to scale your business.
	Research your competitors.
	Test your subscription service.

Chapter 6:
The Art and Science of Attracting Customers to Your Subscription Business

There's no subscription service unless you have subscribers.

Sales Funnel: What It Is and Why You Need It

Study human behavior, and before long, you'll be convinced that our decision-making is a process. When we buy things, we don't always make the purchasing decision instantly. It may take a couple of hours, days, weeks, months, or even years before we decide to buy a specific product or service. Salespeople and marketers have recognized this human tendency and learned how to get it to work for them. From this study came a concept we know as the sales funnel.

We're sure you know how a funnel looks—it's widest at the top and narrowest at the bottom. This shape mimics the journey that subscribers or customers take from becoming aware that a service or product exists up until they buy it. What this means is that the sales process begins with numerous potential prospects. As the process unfolds, the number of prospects decreases until few of them actually buy what you sell. This end point corresponds with the time when you turn a prospect into a subscriber, or they don't buy. Typically, many prospects buy at this stage.

With the invention of the internet, there have been various types of sales funnels created. These funnels come in many different forms, but the ultimate purpose is the same: to lead prospects to a sale with minimal friction. Examples of online funnels include:

- **Membership funnel**: This funnel is ideal for membership-based subscriptions. It's partly why course creators who sell memberships to their online courses like it. It begins when you collect contact details of potential subscribers. This means you'll need to offer a lead magnet. Once you have email subscribers, your next step is to turn them into paid subscribers of the basic plan. Those who purchase the basic plan are later nudged to consider upgrading to the next best membership plan.

- **Product launch funnel**: This type of funnel is great when you introduce your subscription service. You can also employ it when you launch a new feature of your product or service. Its essence is to create excitement about the upcoming product or feature. It starts when a potential subscriber gives you their contact details in exchange for content that shows how the new product or feature will benefit them. The content is often delivered through videos and email. The last email in a series of four or five introduces an early bird that is often the discounted price of the product or feature.

- **Quiz funnel**: This type of funnel suits a situation when you want to offer targeted products or services. For example, if you have multiple subscription boxes, you can use it. Before making offers, a potential subscriber answers a set of questions. Based on their answers, you recommend a specific offer. A good example is when you're a personal trainer and you sell fitness-related subscription boxes. You could ask questions that require the prospect to provide their age, weight, height, and fitness goal. It's advisable to ask a few questions or else the prospect might leave your website.

- **Tripwire funnel**: This is a funnel that begins when you offer a subscription service of high value at a steep discount. The product offered acts as a way to get your foot into the potential subscriber's door. Once they purchase it, you know they value it, and you can offer them your core subscription service. Although the initial offer may not be profitable, it can open the door to earning a lot of money over the life of the subscriber.

- **Webinar funnel**: This funnel is great when you sell high ticket subscription services. Nothing prevents you from using a webinar funnel if LTV warrants it. A webinar is like a live event that's done online. During the webinar, you provide valuable content to participants and make a pitch toward its end. In the old days, marketers wrote books that achieved the same purpose. Today, webinars have replaced those books and are more effective because they're in the much-loved video format. After giving the pitch, you send follow-up emails to convert more of the participants into subscribers. The main advantage of a webinar funnel is that it allows you to showcase your expertise and authority. This is important when you sell anything.

Four Stages of a Sales Funnel

It doesn't matter what type of sales funnel you use because all encompass key stages for successful selling. Your main task is to figure out where in the sales funnel are the majority of your target audience situated. Then, you can choose appropriate marketing channels and present your target audience with the right message. This makes it absolutely necessary to understand these stages of any sales funnel: awareness, interest, decision, and action. You may have heard about AIDA, which is an acronym for these four stages. Let's briefly learn what each of these stages is about:

Stage 1: Awareness

Imagine that you're browsing your friends' Facebook posts when you come across a sponsored post about debt elimination. You look at it for a couple of seconds before you continue browsing your feed. What has just happened is that you were made aware of a brand about debt elimination. From the brand's perspective, you're now aware of their product or service. Many times, this is combined with a landing page to complete the awareness picture. This first stage of a sales funnel when you encounter a product or service is called the awareness level.

A potential subscriber may become aware of your service through numerous ways, including social media posts, blog posts, word of mouth, or online or offline advertising. If they're looking for a solution, they may respond by contacting you. Often, this person will contact you because you've piqued their interest. Once they get in touch with you, they become a lead. Trying to sell your subscription service at this point will cost you a lot more time and money than is necessary.

Stage 2: Interest

At this stage, the lead knows that they need a solution that you can provide. However, they won't immediately buy from you. They'll first conduct more research about you and your brand and competitors to find the best solution. That's why many types of businesses offer the prospect something—a lead magnet—during the awareness stage. This allows these businesses to educate the lead about what they offer and how it can be of value.

The key here is to remember that there's no selling. Your focus is to help the lead in making a decision to do business with you. If you sell at this stage, many of your prospects might go elsewhere to look for a solution. The reason is that they're not yet mentally ready to make a decision about wanting your solution.

Stage 3: Decision

During the third stage of a sales funnel, the lead decides to buy. You want them to buy from you, so you should provide information that sways them to your side. This is where making an irresistible offer (to be discussed later) comes in handy.

Sales pages are the tools to employ in this stage. Not only do sales pages include offers, but they also provide information on why your solution is the best.

Stage 4: Action

All the work you would have done above prepares your lead for this stage. It's time for them to whip out their credit or debit card and buy from you. There's little else you can do at this point.

However, if they don't buy, you can make follow-ups with them. Hopefully, you've collected their contact details.

The Six-Step Process for Creating Your Sales Funnel

Knowing AIDA, it's now the right time to create your own sales funnel. You're fortunate that you've already done the legwork to intimately understand your target audience. That information comes in handy in creating a sales funnel. Your main objective when creating a sales funnel is to convert as many people as possible from one stage of the funnel to the next. Tracking conversions will be key in optimizing your funnel. For now, however, your aim should be to create a working funnel. Optimization will come later.

The steps that you follow when creating a sales funnel are:

Step 1: Create a Lead Magnet

Although we discussed lead magnets earlier, we'd like to offer additional ideas. This step takes advantage of the fact that your target audience is looking for a solution to their problems or methods to achieve what they want. You can help them by creating content that explains how to solve their problem or achieve their goals.

The focus of your lead magnet should squarely be to help your target audience address their problem. Your market research provides plenty of options on what content to create. If you're interested in the raised-bed vegetable gardening niche, you'll find that many people want to know what type of vegetables grow well in raised beds. You can create content that provides answers to this query.

Your lead magnet can be one page of content or more, depending on its type. It's vital to enrich it with relevant content and reduce fluff to zero.

Step 2: Design and Build a Landing Page

We introduced a landing page in Chapter 4. This is the page where you'll tell your prospects how they'll benefit by downloading a lead magnet created above. You can remind yourself about a landing page by revisiting the relevant section in Chapter 4.

Step 3: Send People to Your Landing Page

It's a mistake to think that if you build a landing page, people will flock to it willingly. That's not the case in millions of situations. You need a method to lure people into visiting your landing page.

There are many methods to do this, as explained in Chapter 4. The good thing is that most online advertising platforms guide you on the creation of advertisements. It should therefore be easy to run PPC advertisements. Let us reiterate this point: Irrespective of the platform, set a fixed budget to avoid spending more than you can afford.

Your advertisement should offer the lead magnet to your potential prospects. This means you should tease these people into clicking your advertisement and visiting your landing page.

You can also use social media and blog posts to send traffic to your landing page. The major advantage of social media posts and search engine optimized content is that they don't cost a dime. However, you'll need to spend a lot of time creating the relevant content and posting it. To send prospects to your landing page, include its link in some of your posts. If you're not in a hurry to start generating sales, this approach is your best bet.

Step 4: Craft an Email Campaign

Stages 1 through 3 above are concerned with the awareness stage of your sales funnel. The second a prospect enters their contact details in your landing page and clicks the call to action, they become a lead. You now have their contact details and can start building a rapport with them with the intention of selling your subscription later. We're now in the interest stage of your sales funnel.

Your aim should be to influence the lead into becoming a subscriber to your subscription service. An email campaign is your go-to method for achieving this objective. Do you remember when we talked about an email series when validating your subscription service business idea? An email series is what constitutes an email campaign. Create a similar email series for this stage of your funnel.

Step 5: Make an Offer

You can't turn leads into subscribers unless you make them an offer—an irresistible offer. We provide details of an irresistible offer in the next section, and we suggest going through it before preparing an offer to your subscribers.

Most often, you'll include your offer in a text-based or video sales letter. If you want the best conversion rates, it's worth testing these variations of sales letters. When you make an offer, your leads will make a buying decision. This means that these steps take care of the decision and action stages of your sales funnel.

Step 6: Make Follow-Ups

It's unusual for all your leads to buy the first time you make them an offer. Irrespective of how powerful your email series and offer are, not all leads buy from your first sales pitch. It can take up to eight times of making pitches before a lead buys. Additionally, not all the leads will see your offer email considering that we're all inundated with emails. A typical person can get as many as 120 emails in their mail boxes, which is a lot of emails, and many of them won't be read.

How do you navigate around this difficulty? Simply by making follow-ups. For an online subscription service business, the best method of making follow-ups is by email. This means that you should craft a series of emails targeted at people who don't buy. We've seen top marketers making three to four follow-ups before calling it quits. Use this guide and avoid being like 44% of marketers and salespeople who give up after making just one follow-up. They never realize that they need to make at least five follow-ups to make 80% of their sales.

The bottom line is that you should send follow-up emails. Doing so will likely increase your lead-to-subscriber conversion rate.

How to Measure the Effectiveness of Your Sales Funnel

You've now built your sales funnel and hopefully, are running with it. How do you know that it's doing its intended job? The best method to tell is by measuring the total sales funnel conversion rate. A total conversion rate is the ratio of the total number of sales to the total number of sales leads that you sent the offer to and is expressed in percentages. In formula form,

Total conversion rate = total number of sales/total number of leads x 100

The higher the conversion rate, the harder your sales funnel is working. What happens if the conversion rate is low? By a low conversion rate, we mean that it's lower than the industry average. It's time to optimize it, which begins by investigating where you lose many sales. This is a high-level skill that can be worked on as you progress through your journey.

For now, suffice it to say that the problem with low conversion rates lies somewhere between the top and bottom stages of the funnel. To identify where the major conversion lies, evaluate your email open rates and offer conversion rates. Email open rate tells you how many leads open the emails you send them. This should help you identify how many leads are progressively moving from the interest stage to the action stage of your sales funnel.

The offer conversion rate is the percentage of visitors to your sales letter that become subscribers. Furthermore, it tells you how effective your sales letter and offer are.

The Best Method to Get More Leads Into Your Sales Funnel

A couple of days ago, we wanted an online application that could allow us to draw beautiful charts. After searching, we found one that seemed to be a good fit. For example, it was easy to use, making our learning curve short. We went ahead and created a free account in order to start using it. As we played around with it, we ended up drawing a chart we liked.

We wanted to use the chart offline, which meant that we needed to download it. Unfortunately, when we hit the download button, a pop-up informed us that we need to have a premium account to use that feature. This method, called the freemium model, can be effective in taking leads and turning them into subscribers. The word "freemium" combines two words, "free" and "premium," to indicate that you get paid features at no cost.

It was easy for us to create a free account, allowing us to use some of the features of the app, and leading us to take advantage of a technique called involvement. This approach allows you to have a feeling of owning something and enjoying it. Because it feels like yours, it can be hard to let go of it. That's how we felt about that chart-drawing app. Although we didn't purchase the premium subscription, we learned a great deal about the power of the freemium model.

Offering a freemium model is a powerful method for building relationships with users. This allows you to reduce selling friction when you offer paid-for advanced features. You can use this approach for most internet-based businesses such as in gaming, software, and other services, including in resumé-making.

The freemium model also takes advantage of a person's tendency to want free things. Advertisers and marketers have been using the word "free" for more than 100 years. People cut coupons to get product samples at no cost. At conferences, it's not unusual to spot numerous people lugging free keychains and pens. Samples enable one to use the word "Free" in ads, which will result in more sales. Companies that display their wares at conferences know that they need to attract visitors to their stable. They achieve this, not only by the design of their stable, but by also offering free items.

You, too, can take advantage of this human psychology and get your startup up and running fast.

Pros and Cons of the Freemium Model

The aim of the freemium model for a subscription service is to lure as many users as possible. Once these users start using the service, you can learn a lot about their behavior and fine-tune your methods of selling them advanced features.

Like any business approach, the freemium model not only offers pros but also cons as well.

Pros

- a fast method for acquiring numerous initial users of a subscription service.

- provides a means for a deep study of your target audience and fine-tune your service offering.

- can be used with advertisements to boost revenue.

- it's great to generate brand awareness over a short period of time.

Cons

- You can easily offer too many features, preventing free users from needing to convert to paid users.

- User fatigue on the free version of your service may discourage upgrading.

- It can be hard to convert free users to paid subscribers.

Right here, we should make an important point: The freemium model is not a free trial. First, the freemium model gives free users access for a lifetime, while a free trial has a limited duration. When this deadline comes, a free trialist has to decide whether to buy a paid subscription or forfeit the use of the subscription.

Another key difference is on the amount of features that free users can access. The freemium model offers a limited number of features, while a free trial can provide full or part access to a premium subscription. A free trial often leads to a higher conversion rate than a freemium model. Despite this, as a startup, a freemium model is suitable for you to generate greater awareness. You may then convert to a free trial once you start focusing on increasing conversion rates.

The Most Potent Method to Convert Leads Into Subscribers

The basic premise behind selling your subscription service is having the right solution for your target audience. Then, you can start thinking about ways for potential subscribers to do business with you. A tool you use to get potential subscribers interested in your solution is called an irresistible offer. Combining this type of offer with your value proposition will skyrocket your sales. We've already discussed value propositions elsewhere, and now we turn our attention to an irresistible offer.

What an Irresistible Offer Means

Before we define an irresistible offer, let's understand what we mean by an offer. An offer is what you promise a subscriber that you'll give them in exchange for their money. This immediately means that offers come in many shapes and sizes. Some make potential subscribers waste no time in giving you money while others don't get their attention. An irresistible offer is a downright powerful offer.

An irresistible offer is one that is value-heavy, meaning that the value of your products or services far exceeds the price they pay. When a potential subscriber finds your offer, they don't think twice about buying what you sell—it's a "no-brainer" for them. Let us illustrate such an offer with two examples:

Suppose you have a secondhand Ford F150 that you want to sell because you want to buy a sedan, perhaps a BMW. Luckily, you know what's an irresistible offer and go about creating it. Since your truck is still in pristine condition, you set its price at $20,000—a slightly higher price compared to similar vehicles. You'd agree that selling this car won't be easygoing due to its price. You tip the scales of selling it to your favor by introducing elements that make it more attractive to potential buyers than its rivals. For example, you can offer its potential buyer the following:

- one full tank of gasoline each month for the next six months

- a chance to drive the car for two weeks and to return it if they don't like it

- one free service for the first year of ownership

- a 12-month guarantee on mechanical and electrical parts

To make each of the above elements powerful, consider adding a reason why you're offering it. For example, you may say that you're offering the two-week test drive because the vehicle is easy to drive, comfortable, and gets tough jobs done. Most importantly, this offer must be targeted at the right audience.

For the second example, let's consider a name-brand gadget subscription box you send out quarterly. Imagine that you want to promote this box hard in the next two months. What type of offer can you put together for your potential subscribers? Because you understand your target subscribers, you decide to add the following items in the upcoming box: PaleBlue USB batteries, Beads Studio buds, a Syntech USB B to USB C adapter pack, a Sandisk 128GB ultra flair USB 3.0 flash drive, and a Belkin 8" by 9" mouse pad.

Your irresistible offer could include a guarantee for each item in the box, a warranty, and a discount on the whole box. A good way to discount that works well is stating the retail price of each item in the box, and then stating your discounted price. For example, if the total price is X dollars, you can offer the box cheaper at Y dollars. Explaining why you're making a discount is important because people always want to have a logical reason for buying something.

Strategies for Creating an Irresistible Offer

There must be a method behind the creation of an irresistible offer. Otherwise, you can lose money and go out of business. The creation of an irresistible offer is preceded by thorough market and audience research, which is what you should have done already. Each of the strategies you use must be aimed at increasing the perceived value of your subscription service.

Understand this: When you solicit subscribers, you don't have to make money in the front-end. By front-end, we mean the first sale you make. The purpose of this sale is to get your subscriber to sample your subscription service with the aim of making profit later.

When you combine the applicable strategies we'll discuss below, your offer will truly become irresistible. Here are the strategies to consider implementing:

- **Toss in an extra item or two**. Do you want to charge a full price upfront for your subscription service? There's nothing wrong in doing so. However, you may be stopping some potential subscribers from making the buying decision because of price. You can influence these people by adding one or two extra items to increase the perceived value of your offer. For example, if you're offering a raised-bed vegetable gardening subscription box, you may include a free e-book or online course with it.

When you use this strategy, your profit margin stays the same because you don't change the price of your subscription service. This strategy works great if you can deliver the extra items you add without increasing your costs. Online courses and e-books work great. The good news is that you don't have to have your own e-book or online course to add them to your subscription service. There are many sources of private label rights websites that allow you to download e-books and video courses for free or for a small fee. This means you don't even have to be a writer to offer these types of products. The key is making sure that the extra item adds value to your potential subscribers.

- **Add a potent risk reversal**. No one wants to take risks when buying products or services. You don't want to take risks and your potential subscriber doesn't either. However, one of you must take most of the risk for a transaction to occur between the two of you. If your potential subscriber feels that they're taking the most risk, they won't buy. To convert such prospects into subscribers, you instead assume most of the risk. If the prospect believes they have nothing to lose by buying your subscription service, you're going to make a lot more sales than without assuming the risk.

There are multiple methods for assuming risk, including giving money-back guarantees and warranties, or delivering the product or service first before the subscriber pays. Let's briefly go deeper into each of these three methods.

- o **Money-back guarantee**: If you've paid attention to offers you've received in recent times, you may have noticed they included money-back guarantees. Typically, you'll see a 30-day, 60-day, or 12-month money-back guarantee. For regular products or services, the longer the money-back guarantee, the lower the likelihood the customer would request their money back.

  In subscription services, it's a good idea to set money-back guarantees that match the length of each subscription. For instance, if subscribers renew their subscriptions monthly, the money-back guarantee should be 30 days. If you're absolutely confident about your subscription, you could offer a double-your-money-back guarantee. This means that if the subscription is $50, you give them $100 if they're unhappy about it and want a refund. This is what a potent risk reversal means.

- **Free trial.** In the 1960s, the late legendary copywriter, Eugene Schwartz, wrote an advertisement titled *Don't Pay a Penny Till This Course Turns You Into a Mental Magnet.* He stated his offers as follows:

  > Just mail in the enclosed FREE TRIAL coupon today! This wonder-working course will immediately be sent to you without cost, obligation, or pre-payment of any kind. Try it for [10] full days entirely at our risk. At the end of that time, if (as we believe) you are completely delighted, then send us the low cost of only $9.98. If, on the other end, you are disappointed in this course in any way—if it does not live up to every one of the claims we have made for it on this page, then simply return it to us, and owe nothing!

  This is an example of a free trial offer that has become popular in SaaS businesses. It's a great way to take 100% of the risk and the subscriber has nothing to lose for taking you up on the offer. A free trial for SaaS usually opens up access to features typically reserved for paid subscribers. Businesses behind them already know that a certain number of trialists will convert into paying subscribers within the trial period of 7, 14, or 30 days. If your subscription service suits this type of risk reversal, implement it as soon as possible.

- **Offer results in advance**: A variation of a free trial is the results in advance risk reversal technique. In this case, the subscriber pays a portion of the subscription fee, uses the subscription for a given period, and if they get promised results, they pay the remaining amount. If they're disappointed with the results, they don't pay the balance.

- ○ **Include a warranty**. This approach is great when your subscription service includes physical products such as electronics and software. You can tell subscribers that your electronics have a 12-month warranty that covers defects.

- **Bundle subscriptions**. Your potential subscribers don't only want your type of subscription; they also can use others that complement yours. For instance, if you create a streaming music subscription, your subscribers may likely enjoy having access to a movie streaming subscription or something similar. Bundling these subscriptions will not only save your subscriber money, but increase your revenue per subscriber. Automakers or dealerships can bundle car subscriptions with insurance or maintenance subscriptions.

- **Offer sound discounts**. What makes Black Friday and Christmas great times for selling things? It's because many retailers and businesses offer sales promotions that are often discounted. Since people like bargains, they buy items on sale in droves. However, you should only discount a subscription service that subscribers want. To make your discounted offer effective, include urgency to get potential subscribers to act. For example, you can say that your subscription service is available at a 25% discount for five days only.

Remember that discounting doesn't always work because people have a tendency to think that a cheap item is of inferior quality. Sometimes you should increase prices and see what happens, especially if you offer a highly perceived value.

Don't rush when creating an irresistible offer. Think it through and test it on 100 or so potential subscribers to determine if it works or not.

Checklist

	Determine which online funnel will suit your business and subscribers.
	Finalize your lead magnet.
	Finalize your website.
	Create advertisements leading to your landing page.
	Finalize your email strategy and campaign.
	Find a good balance of following up with your subscribers.
	Try different methods to capture leads.
	Determine what freebies and samples you can offer without skimping on quality or affecting your value perception.

Chapter 7:

Strategies to Retain Subscribers

The holy grail of succeeding in a subscription service business—or any business—is to retain subscribers or customers. There are powerful reasons for this that we'll discuss in this chapter. We will also define subscriber retention rate and churn rate to help in understanding them. Most importantly, we'll provide strategies for attaining and maintaining a high customer retention rate and low churn rate.

What Is Subscriber Retention Rate and How Does It Differ From Churn Rate?

Two terms that we should first define before we understand subscriber retention rate and churn rate are subscriber retention and churn. We'll first explain subscriber retention and its corresponding rate.

Subscriber retention defines how well a subscription service business retains its subscribers. The metric that measures how well a subscription service retains subscribers is known as subscriber retention rate. You determine your subscriber retention rate as follows:

$SR = (TS - NS)/S$ x 100, where

SR - subscriber retention rate

TS - total number of subscribers at the end of a given period

NS - total number of new subscribers acquired over the same period

S - total number of subscribers at the start of the period of interest

Suppose that you start a certain month with 43 subscribers, acquire 10 new subscribers during that month, and end the month with 47 subscribers. Your subscriber retention rate at the end of that month is:

$$SR = (TS - NS)/S \times 100$$

$$= (47 - 10)/43 \times 100$$

$$= 86.0\%$$

Is this subscriber retention rate good or not? It's hard to say without comparing it with a benchmark, which can be an industry reference or your subscriber retention goal. If it beats your benchmark, then your subscriber retention rate is good.

You should recognize that you need to have a benchmark subscriber retention rate before you start measuring yours. The quickest method for establishing your benchmark is to find the industry average of your niche and then set your own target. When you set the target, remember to pass it through the SMART test. This means that your target subscriber retention rate should be specific (S), measurable (M), achievable (A), realistic (R), and time-bound (T). What you consider achievable and realistic is up to you, but ensure that you don't overextend yourself and set yourself up for failure. Rather, be conservative initially and progressively challenge yourself with stretch targets.

Another crucial point is that you should chart and evaluate the trend of subscriber retention rates you get. This helps you measure progress against yourself—and not others or a goal you set. That way, you can tell if you're making progress or regressing. If the trend heads downward, you can find out what's the cause and figure out how to stop and improve it.

Let's now turn our attention to churn and churn rate. When subscribers leave a subscription service business, we call that churn. The percentage of subscribers who cancel subscriptions over a given period is called the churn rate or attrition rate. Mathematically, you calculate the churn rate by using this formula:

$$CR = SC/S \times 100, \text{ where}$$

CR - churn rate

SC - total number of subscribers who have canceled their subscription during a given period

S - total number of subscribers at the start of the period of interest

If during a given month 7 subscribers cancel their subscriptions and you started with 47 subscribers, then the churn rate is:

$$CR = SC/S \times 100$$

$$= 7/47 \times 100$$

$$= 14.9\%$$

You'll agree that calculating the churn rate this way is simple. There are other formulas used to calculate the churn rate, but they tend to be complicated. It's best to go for simple calculation and measure the churn rate over a period of time. This will give you a trend that tells a story you can do something about. As with the subscriber retention rate, it's worth having a benchmark against which to gauge your churn rates.

What Causes High Subscriber Churn Rates?

Measuring and analyzing your churn rates is one of the most important activities in your subscription service business. You can quickly identify exceedingly high churn rates and start an investigation to unearth the causes. Unless you find the cause of high churn rates, your business's revenue will decline. To help you with finding possible causes of high churn rates, we discuss the top five reasons that may apply to your business.

1. Low Level of Subscriber Engagement

A subscriber begins interacting with your business from the moment they first encounter your brand. This may be from your blog posts,

PPC advertising, or through any number of ways. How you interact with them influences not only whether they become a subscriber, but also if they stay with your business after becoming a subscriber.

Typically, businesses give a lot of effort to ensure they attract subscribers, but drop the ball post-subscription stage. They barely answer subscriber questions that may be raised through social media, forums, or websites. There's no way that subscribers could become loyal to your business if you act this way. Instead, they start detaching and finally, cut any link with you, increasing your churn rate.

2. Attracting the Wrong Subscribers

Subscription service businesses—and any business for that matter—generally put their best foot forward when attracting subscribers. The excitement you inject in your copy can influence subscribers who aren't the best fit for your business. Irrespective of how great your service is, such subscribers will unsubscribe in no time after joining.

In certain cases, subscribers may purchase your subscription not because of your fault, but because they didn't fully understand what you offer. Either way, we can't expect those subscribers to stick with you.

Your best bet is to nail down your messaging and make sure that it's specific and calls out your target audience, if need be. Additionally, use simple language to describe the features and benefits of your subscription service.

3. Subscribers Aren't Nailing Their Objectives

Subscribers want results, and if they don't get them, they unsubscribe and try elsewhere—your competition. The features and benefits of your subscription service don't mean much if your subscribers aren't getting the results you promise. It may not be your fault, but you should be concerned because it negatively impacts your revenue. You have every reason to find out how to help your subscribers achieve their subscription goals.

It's not unusual for subscribers to receive their goods or get access to their online subscription and still not follow-through. There are many contributors to this situation, including the excitement of getting a new thing. Once the excitement dies, the enthusiasm dies and we forget, or rather, we shelve the goods as they come. This phenomenon is common in the online courses world. Just one student finishes an online course out of every 10, which is a dismal completion rate.

Many factors are responsible for the failure of subscribers to reach their goals. One of the reasons for this is poor subscription user experience or their inability to understand how to use the subscription or products. This is where an improvement in your onboarding process can be a lifesaver. We've discussed how to onboard new subscribers successfully and we refer you to that section.

4. Expired Credit Cards

Have you ever decided to renew a manual subscription service and failed to do so? That often happens, as does the failure to renew your credit card. When it has expired, the affected subscriber can't renew their subscription, which is a phenomenon known as delinquent churn. We know that this doesn't appear to be your baby, but you should consider it so. The reason is that it negatively affects your business and you can do something about it.

Your go-to solution is automated dunning software. With this technology, as explained earlier, you contact the subscriber to let them know about the situation and what to do about it. It's also true that credit card issuers may remind their customers to renew their cards but taking responsibility is a proactive move—not a reactive one. Don't worry about the possibility of your subscriber canceling their subscription: They're on their way to do so at any rate if you don't do something about it. If you offer what they want, they will renew.

5. Service Not Meeting Expectations Anymore

Every subscriber wants value for their money. There are times when they may feel that your service doesn't tick this box for them anymore and they unsubscribe. Some factors that lead to this kind of cancellation, such as your subscriber budget, are beyond your control. However, you can do something to ensure that your subscription stays relevant to your subscribers.

The main initiative to combat this is innovation. You should seek ways to improve your subscription service so that it stays relevant with changing times and the wants of your subscribers. That's why conducting regular subscriber surveys is crucial. It'll help you identify the needs and wants of your subscribers and react quickly to satisfy them.

Staying on top of the above-mentioned issues will go a long way toward improving your subscription service's churn rate. Automatically, your subscriber retention rates will improve as will your revenue and profitability.

Why Retain Subscribers in Your Subscription Service Business

A business that tries to thrive by continually acquiring new customers or subscribers is bound to have profitability issues. However, if they retain customers or subscribers, they reap a multitude of benefits. We'd like to discuss those benefits so that you can see how valuable this activity is, and hopefully, make it a part of your subscription service business.

Increased Free Marketing

Subscribers won't stay with you unless you provide them with delightful experiences. Some of the ways for retaining subscribers that we've already talked about include seamless onboarding. Imagine that you've onboarded a set of subscribers so that they're happy with your service. You also provided them with tips to benefit the most from your service and they get the results you promised. What do you think they'll likely do?

Typically, they'll head to their favorite social media platform and brag about their experiences with your service. Some, if not many, will happily share their experiences with friends, family, and colleagues. It's not unusual for some of your subscribers to also refer new subscribers to you. If you've made it a point to ask for testimonials, you'll get more of them than you can use on your website. What do these activities have in common? They market your business without you spending a dime—it's free marketing.

If you've not yet become aware of it, your subscribers have followers online and offline. Some of those people value the opinions of your subscribers. This means that when your subscribers share their experiences about your service, their followers, friends, and family may also want to have the same experiences. The way to have such experiences is to buy and test drive your service. Best of all, the subscribers you acquire this way are likely to stay with your business for longer.

There are many more benefits for getting referrals, including the following:

- **Your business will attract high-value subscribers**. If we trust you and you recommend a product or service to us, we're likely to try it. Most importantly, we won't conduct as much background research as we would if we were hiring a stranger. The level of trust we'll have for you is higher. 92% of consumers trust you if they know you. Trust is crucial for getting new subscribers, meaning that referred potential subscribers are likely to do business with you. Additionally, such subscribers will, in turn, refer others and the domino effect will continue.

- **You'll generate higher conversion rates**. You'll recall that people who enter your sales funnel at the top barely know you. As a result, you'll have to nurture them to build trust before converting them into subscribers. Not only does this take time, it also takes patience. However, people referred by others won't enter your sales funnel at the top. Perhaps they might start engaging with you at the middle to the bottom of your funnel because they already trust you. This explains why such people are four times more likely to buy than those who start at the top of your sales funnel. Many of those people will convert to subscribers than those who start your sales funnel at the top. Conversion rates from referred consumers can be up to three to five times higher than those obtained when using other marketing channels.

- **Increased brand awareness**. When your subscribers share their experiences with others, they help raise the awareness of your brand. If consumers notice that your brand is helping others in ways they wish for themselves, they may consider finding out about it. This may include trialing your subscription service to confirm that you indeed provide excellent subscriber experiences. It'll be up to you to convert these trialists into subscribers.

- **Improved subscriber retention rates**. It shouldn't be a surprise that referred consumers are more loyal considering that they trust you. This loyalty translates to a higher retention rate. When a consumer is referred to your brand, they may result in a 37% higher subscriber retention rate.

The benefits mentioned above should get you excited to pay attention to subscriber retention. Investing in subscriber retention will pay you back in spades for your time and effort.

It's Affordable to Retain Subscribers

Acquiring new subscribers requires time, effort, and money. If you don't retain subscribers and want to grow your business, you'll need to increase each of these resources. As a result, it becomes expensive to acquire subscribers. As stated already, you can pay anywhere between 5 to 25 times more to acquire a new subscriber than retaining one. This means that it's cheaper to retain subscribers, which improves your business profitability. Retaining subscribers allows you to channel these resources to the growth of your business.

There are a couple of reasons why it's more affordable to retain subscribers. When marketing to them, you don't have to start from the brand awareness level but way down near the bottom of the funnel. This means it takes a shorter time to convert them into subscribers and consequently, it costs less. Another reason is that you know their desires and pains well enough to influence them to buy. There's very little trial and error to do, which means your marketing is much more effective. It's no wonder the probability of selling to a new consumer is 5–20% compared to 60–70% when selling to an existing one.

Improved Return on Investment

As a business owner, you're also an investor in your venture. Every investor wants their money to work the hardest for them. One way of measuring how hard your money is working in your business is to use a metric called return on investment (ROI). You determine ROI by taking the ratio of profit from your investment to the amount you invested and express the results in percentage.

In math terms, ROI = Profit from investment/cost of the investment.

For the same cost of investment, an increased profit leads to a higher ROI. This is what you get when you retain subscribers because of lower subscriber acquisition costs. If you increase subscriber retention by 5%, you can increase ROI by between 25% and 95%, which is significant. You can double the jump in your ROI by raising your subscriber retention by 10%, which is doable if you know how. We'll provide you with the "how" below.

Retained Subscribers Are a Source of Business Improvement Ideas

For subscription businesses, innovation is a must. One of the ways to innovate is to ask for subscriber feedback. When you have many retained subscribers, you have collaborators you can trust. As a result, when you ask for business improvement ideas, you'll get them in numbers.

Not only will this increase your chances of coming up with improved processes, products, or services, but it'll also strengthen the relationship you already have with your subscribers. In turn, this will result in solid subscriber retention rates coupled with the benefits mentioned above. Most importantly, implement the ideas that your subscribers provide and give them feedback. Remember that subscription service businesses are about the customer, not anyone else.

Higher Subscriber LTV

Subscriber retention is one area that can increase your subscriber LTV. As subscribers stay longer with you, they buy more from your business and are likely to purchase more subscriptions. It's easier for your subscribers to buy from you because it's a lot of work to find a business that delivers excellent subscriber experiences. The only time they'll not purchase more from you is if you don't have what they want. Consequently, your subscriber LTV will be higher than if they stayed with you for a short period. Additionally, your profitability will receive a boost, as does your ROI as explained above.

Do you think it's worth working your butt off to retain subscribers judging by the benefits above? We think it's worth every effort if succeeding in your subscription service business matters. That's why we've added the next section.

How to Keep Engaging Your Subscribers and Retain Them

You learned above that subscriber engagement is key to curbing high churn rates and maintaining desired subscriber retention. It can be overwhelming as a newbie subscription service business owner to know what to do. We'd like to offer you actionable ideas that, when implemented, will help you engage subscribers and achieve your target subscriber retention rates and revenue.

Create and Send Your Service's Email Newsletter Frequently

One of the simple means of engaging your subscribers is by communicating with them through an email newsletter. The great news is that email newsletters are cost-effective because they can be automated by using email automation software. Think of a newsletter as a means of keeping your subscribers abreast with the latest news, updates to your subscriptions, or to deliver tips and techniques related to their subscriptions.

It's not a good idea to send an email newsletter for the sake of ticking a "sent newsletter" box. Your email newsletter should be worth opening and reading and have a purpose behind it. Are you sending the newsletter to update your subscribers about your service, or do you want them to read a certain blog? Before you sit down to craft the headline of your newsletter, first work out why you want to send it. The reason is that you want your email newsletter to be short enough to have a chance of being read.

An effective newsletter has the following components:

- **A read-me headline**: How do you decide to read some emails and leave others unread? If you've never thought about this before, open your email box right now. Pick five emails that you feel compelled to read. What criteria did you use to make your choices? We can promise you that you, yourself, read emails whose headlines have caught your attention. Perhaps you also chose emails that come from someone you personally know or from a company that has awarded you a contract. Whatever the criteria you used, you didn't open the email to decide whether to read it or not—you decided what email to open based on the headline. Make your headlines relevant to your target market; include a promise for news and curiosity.

- **Get straight to the point**. Tell your subscribers why they should read your newsletter. It's best to tell them how they're going to benefit by reading the email.

- **Link to detailed information you want to share with your subscribers**. There's no need to write the entirety of the content you want your subscribers to know about. Rather, link to blog posts, news posts, or other content you want them to read in detail.

- **Focus on content, not selling**. People dislike being pitched aggressively. Use your email newsletter to add value to your subscribers, not as a sales letter. You can still link to products you want to sell, but this should not be the primary objective of your newsletter.

Don't forget to measure the success rates of your email newsletters. The best metric you can track is click-through rate, which tells you how many emails were opened. Also, track the opening of the links included in your email newsletter.

Accept Mistakes and Apologize

Mistakes can happen, especially when you least expect it. For example, you may accidentally double charge a couple of subscribers in a certain month. You can imagine how angry such a subscriber would be if they found out the error first! Perhaps you may become a victim of cybercrime in which cyber thieves steal your subscribers' data. What do you do in such circumstances?

First, you need to realize that what has happened cannot be undone. However, the results of some mistakes can be reversed. For instance, if you double-charge subscribers, you can reverse one of the transactions. Subscribers need more than reversing or correcting mistakes for them to have confidence in your subscription service. What they need is an apology and assurance that you'll prevent similar mistakes from reoccurring.

The second thing to do is to send an apology to all affected subscribers. In your apology, include details of what transpired and possibly, why it happened. Most importantly, detail what you're doing or have done to prevent the problem or mistake from reoccurring. This reassures your subscribers that you care, and many will stay with your business when they realize this, as long as they're loyal.

We recommend you apologize as soon as possible. After all, it doesn't cost money to apologize.

Inform Your Subscribers About Price Changes Timely

Subscribers, like many types of consumers, are sensitive about the prices of services or goods. Part of the reason is that some of them have tight budgets. A research study discovered that three in five Americans spend all their income each month. Among them, 20% battle to pay their bills, which should be a worry if your subscribers fall into this group. Living from paycheck to paycheck isn't reserved for low-income earners. 9 in 20 of those who earned $100,000 or more were found to live from paycheck to paycheck.

During times of high inflation, such as in 2022, the cost of living is high. This can easily destabilize your subscribers' finances and negatively impact your revenue.

It's crucial to optimize your subscription plans, but make sure that while increasing prices, it doesn't backfire. When ramping up prices, realize that some subscribers may cancel their subscriptions due to being financially overstretched. Again, it's vital to elevate your prices in line with your understanding of your subscribers. Carrying out a survey consistently, say quarterly, might help you decide how to increase your pricing.

While speaking about pricing, also pay attention to what your competitors are charging for the same subscription service. This alone can result in subscribers churning if your competitor offers the same service at a lower price.

When you change your prices, don't keep your subscribers in the dark about it. No subscriber will be happy to see their credit card being charged a higher subscription fee without their knowledge. Write to your subscribers in good time and tell them about price changes and why they happened. This will be easy to do when you stick to your mission.

Capitalize on Subscriber Testimonials and Their Stories

Strange as it may sound, we rarely want to be pioneers. We would rather choose to follow the lead of others, although we often do so unconsciously. This is uncomfortably true, but we have to first realize this when building our businesses. When you determine something as correct based on what others think, social proof is at play.

You can take advantage of the social proof idea to influence existing subscribers to upgrade or to maintain their subscriptions. All it takes is deliberately asking and collecting subscriber testimonials and displaying them prominently in your marketing collateral. You can take this a step further and ask for subscriber stories that show how they transformed after using your subscription. You can share these stories with other subscribers through your newsletter.

Create a Community Around Your Subscription Service

Why do you think many businesses create communities such as forums and Facebook groups? The answer is that they know they can tap into social proof and also minimize the number of subscriber support tickets. It's the first benefit of communities that should interest you the most regarding subscriber retention.

A community is a great place to share resources with your subscribers on how best to use your service. We've already indicated earlier that subscribers can churn if they don't get the expected results. When you purchase a subscription service, you use it alone. If it seems like it's taking longer for the results to come, you develop doubts. Add to this the fact that if we're inundated with subscription service offers, we're likely to churn, as we likely won't get the results we expect. With a community, you and your subscribers can allay any fears others have that your subscription service doesn't work.

The second advantage of communities is that they create a sense of belonging for your subscribers. Although we live in an interconnected world, loneliness is real. People experiencing loneliness can suffer from physical and mental health effects. A community makes subscribers feel they belong to something worthy, and they're likely to stick to your service if you provide a thriving and enthusiastic community.

Create a Personalized User Experience

Your subscribers may have purchased the same subscription service but expect it to help them solve unique problems or achieve specific goals. For instance, your subscribers may have different time pressures or may have subscribed to different plans. It's, therefore, necessary to provide subscriber-tailored solutions. This means you don't work with subscribers as a group but as individuals.

Providing personalized solutions will help with trust building and enhancing subscriber loyalty. Research data corroborates this idea when it found that 80% of consumers prefer to purchase from businesses that offer personalization. Additionally, 90% of them are heavily influenced by personalization.

The foundation of personalization is understanding your subscribers' pain points, needs, and wants. That's why we placed researching the market immediately below generating a business idea in Chapter 4. Your subscriber needs and wants guide nearly all the activities that you perform in a subscription service business. Next in importance, you should consistently evaluate the data you generate throughout the period a subscriber does business with you.

Some of the ways you can introduce personalization are by allowing preferred payment methods, order customization, delivery times, frequency of receiving emails, and what emails to receive. Don't forget to provide options to pause, cancel, or skip subscriptions.

Create and Regularly Update a Subscriber Communication Calendar

You have a choice of whether to be reactive or proactive regarding subscriber communication. It's either you primarily wait for subscribers to engage with you, or you initiate conversations. Being reactive might work if you have active subscribers, but they'll eventually tire out. A big disadvantage for your business is that you lose control over the communication with subscribers if you're reactive.

It's much better if you're the one who initiates the engagements with subscribers. Because of the frequent times you'll need to communicate with subscribers, you need both a plan and a communication calendar. A communication calendar helps you track your conversations with subscribers.

When you create a communication calendar, keep the following in mind:

- **Have a communication objective**: Each messaging piece to your subscribers should be backed up by a given objective. For instance, you may send a communication message to remind subscribers to renew their credit card details when they expire.

- **Include content production timelines**: A communication calendar's major benefit is that it helps you remember to send a particular message to subscribers. That's why it's essential to add production timelines to all content you want to send to your subscribers. This will also provide a visual picture of the work that needs to be done to achieve a particular goal.

- **Communication channels to use**: Effective communication requires three elements: the sender of a message, the receiver, and the medium. Your calendar should include the medium to use to reach your subscribers.

When your communication calendar is set, it's time to start preparing your messaging.

Provide an Option to Downgrade

We understand that subscription service businesses make the most revenue when subscribers opt for top and premium plans. However, being solely focused on upselling subscribers to these plans may not necessarily be the best move. You might try to upsell a subscriber who doesn't need the top-of-the-range subscription plan. Alternatively, you might attempt to retain a subscriber who's barely managing to stay subscribed to your top plan. This is unlikely to work.

Your best bet is to offer a downgrade option. It may appear like you'll be losing revenue by doing this. When you consider that a subscriber may be looking to cancel their subscription, offering them a downgrade isn't a bad idea. Besides, you may still be able to run your subscription service at your desired average LTV. Best of all, the subscriber who downgrades is still a ripe target for future upselling.

Now that you know what to do to retain subscribers, it's time to implement quick-win ideas. It's even better to build your subscription service so that it supports the above subscriber-engagement-and-retaining ideas.

Checklist

	Track your subscription and retention rates.
	Compare monthly analytics to inform new strategies and innovations.
	Ensure that you engage your customers at regular intervals and tweak your strategies if needed.
	Adjust your messaging so that you attract the subscribers you want.
	Request feedback from your subscribers to see where you can improve and where you may be missing the mark.
	Create a community around your service on social media or online forums.
	Personalize your customer's experience and be proactive in communication rather than reactive.

Plan for and provide options to downgrade or pause subscriptions.

Chapter 8:

How to Measure the Financial Performance of Your Subscription Service Business

How do you determine if your subscription service is successful or not? The same way you establish the success of every business—by reading its financial statements. Within each financial statement, you find metrics such as profit margin, debt-to-equity ratio, and return-on-equity (ROE). There's a difference between how you read finances for traditional businesses versus subscription service businesses.

This chapter prepares you to understand the finances for subscription service businesses. Once subscription services' finances make sense, you'll be ready to evaluate your business's performance. Most importantly, you'll know what levers to operate to improve the performance of your subscription service business. We'll focus mainly on the income statement.

Introduction to the Finances of Subscription Services

Finances for subscription service businesses are a relatively new thing. That's why the foundation of understanding the finances of subscription service businesses is knowing the terminology. Let's begin by introducing you to financial terms you'll encounter throughout this chapter. One point to note is that not all terms we will define are part of Generally Accepted Accounting Principles (GAA) or International Financial Reporting System (IFRS). Neither are these terms included when reporting to the government. Our focus is not on how you adhere to GAAP or IFRS, but on achieving operational excellence. Let's get started with defining our terms.

- **Annual revenue per user (ARPU):** This is the total recurring income you receive per user or subscriber. Simply divide your annual recurring revenue by the number of subscribers you had during the year. For instance, if your annual revenue is $550,000 and you had 12,000 subscribers, then the ARPU is $45.83 ($550,000/12,000 = $45.83). Exclude one-time fees when figuring out recurring revenue.

- **Monthly recurring revenue (MRR):** This is a measure of revenue you expect to generate each month. It's a useful metric for financial forecasting and for measuring growth from one month to the next. You calculate MRR by multiplying the ARPU by the number of subscribers and dividing the result by 12. In math form, MRR = ARPU x number of subscribers/12 or MRR = ARR/12, depending on what data you have. Taking the above example further, the MRR is $41,667 ($550,000/12 = 41,667).

- **Annual recurring revenue (ARR):** This measures recurring revenue over a year. You obtain it by annualizing MRR—multiplying MRR by 12. If you want to know how your subscription service has been performing over a year, you use ARR.

- **Subscriber ROI:** Knowing how hard your investment is working requires measuring ROI. For this calculation, you need the subscriber acquisition cost and LFV. Dividing LFV by subscriber acquisition cost gives you subscriber ROI. For instance, if it costs $200 to acquire a subscriber who has an LFV of $1,300, the ROI will be 6.5:1. With such a high ROI, you could be spending little money and missing out on growing your company. It's a better position to be in than one where ROI is less than a ratio of 1:1.

Understanding a Subscription Service's Income Statement

An income statement, also known as the profit and loss statement, for traditional businesses shows revenues, expenses, and profits (or losses). You can't run a business successfully if you don't know whether it makes or loses money. Using the income statement, you can compare the success of your business with that of your peers, measure the effectiveness of management, and evaluate the efficacy of business operations. Traditional businesses also use two other financial statements to measure their performance: the balance sheet and statement of cash flows or cash flow statement. We won't discuss the balance sheet, but we'll touch on the statement of cash flows shortly.

The main components of an income statement for a traditional business are:

- **Revenue**: The first part of an income statement is revenue, also called sales. It's recorded for business activities that take place over a given period, such as a month, quarter, or year.

- **Cost of goods sold (COGS)**: It costs money to generate revenue. This expense is called COGS because it takes into account the costs of producing goods or services. It also includes the cost of products you source from suppliers for resale. COGS excludes costs which are not linked with the production of goods and services, such as overhead costs.

- **Gross profit**: This is the difference between revenue and COGS during a given time period. It tells you how efficient you are at converting the costs of direct labor into revenue. You want it to be as high as possible. For financial analysis, we usually divide gross profit by revenue and multiply the result by 100 to measure the effectiveness of COGS management.

- **Expenses**: This is a crucial category of an income statement because it can determine how profitable the business is. It includes operating expenses such as sales commissions, advertising costs, and payroll. Advertising costs are often bundled with administrative expenses in a section called sales, general & administrative (SG&A) expenses. Advertising costs are expenses incurred to bring in new customers using offline and online media advertisements. Administrative costs include expenses such as travel, salaries, and office supplies.

- **Gains**: A business may sell some of its assets during a given period. This money isn't recognized as revenue but as a gain.

For example, a company may sell an unused old vehicle or real estate property to generate cash flow. Activities that generate gains are called non-operating or non-business activities.

- **Losses**: Money may flow out of the business due to non-operating activities. For instance, a business might have been fined for breaking some law. That cost will appear in this part of an income statement.

- **Depreciation**: This is a non-cash expense that occurs when a company distributes the cost of an asset over a given period of time. Only the portion assumed to be the used value of an asset is recorded per given time period.

- **Interest**: This is an expense incurred for borrowing funds from traditional sources, such as banks.

- **Earnings before tax (EBT)**: This is a derived component of an income statement. It measures the profit generated before accounting for taxes. You simply subtract total expenses from gross profit to get EBT.

- **Net income**: Also called earnings, this is what's commonly known as the bottom-line of an income statement. You calculate it by subtracting taxes from EBT.

Here's an example of a traditional income statement:

Fictitious Corporation Income Statement Year ended December 31	
	(in thousands of US dollars)
Revenue	$400
Cost of goods sold	311.56
Gross profit	**88.44**
Selling and operating expenses	54.67

General & administrative expenses	9.65
Total operating expenses	**64.32**
Operating income	**24.12**
Gains/losses	0
Interest expense	0.2
Earnings before taxes	23.92
Earnings tax expense	5.56
Net income	**18.36**

With an understanding of how an income statement for a traditional business looks, let's turn our attention to the income statement of a subscription service business. But first, here is the general equation of a subscription service company:

ARR_n - Churn + ACV = ARR_{n+1}, where

ARR_n - the ARR at the start of a given period

Churn - ARR that you lose due to subscribers canceling their subscriptions

ACV - Annual contract value, a figure that shows the value of a subscriber over a year period that includes upgrades and new subscribers. It can be normalized to a month or quarter by dividing it by 12 or 4, respectively.

We must reemphasize that all the metrics above measure recurring income or costs. Looking at the above formula, it's clear that a subscription service is focused on the future, not the past like a traditional business, as shown in the example statement above. The above formula dictates the components of a subscription service's income statement, which are:

- **ARR**: The top and bottom lines are all recurring revenues. The beginning figure is the ARR at the start of a given period, telling us how much revenue to expect going forward. In a traditional business, your revenue is like a rearview mirror because it tells you how much money you brought in. It might be helpful but it tells you little about what the future holds— that is, how much money you'll make in the next period. Instead of net income as the bottom-line, we end with the ARR that projects what income we can expect in the next period.

  A traditional business needs to perform extra work to figure out what revenue and net income it'll generate in the next period. The problem with this is that you can use any type of assumption to produce forecasts that please you and other stakeholders. ARR is expected money you can rely on, since a properly run subscription service company generates predictable income.

- **Churn**: When we say a subscription service business's revenue is predictable, we don't mean that it stays the same from one period to the next. Recurring revenue can change because you lose some subscribers, get new ones, and upsell others. However, even when it changes, you can project a new ARR fairly easily. Loss of subscribers, which we've called churn all along, is real. You can do all you can but you're going to lose subscribers. We've discussed at length strategies and techniques for minimizing churn, without getting rid of it completely. Churn is what's going to reduce the ARR that you start a given period with. For example, if you start with a $5 million ARR and churn reduces that by $0.25m, you remain with $4.75 million, which is net ARR. Luckily, you can do something to claw back some of your losses due to churn.

- **Recurring expenses**: We wish you could pocket all that $4.75 million at the end of the next period but that's not the case. You need to spend to provide service to your subscribers. Since these costs are essential for delivering your subscription and providing subscriber service, your expenses will include COGS and SG&A. Moreover, you'll need to perform research and development (R&D) to ensure your subscribers get the best service so that they can stick with you. Technically, R&D should be an overhead cost but it's simpler to bundle these costs together to determine the amount needed to service your ARR.

- **Recurring profit margin**: The difference between ARR and recurring costs results in your recurring profit margin. You can represent recurring profit margin as a dollar figure or as a percentage of ARR to determine how well you manage expenses. Recurring profit margin tells you how profitable your subscription service business is. The reason for this is that there's predictability in both your ARR and recurring revenue. When you evaluate how well your subscription business is performing, first check your recurring profit margin.

- **Sales and marketing costs**: These costs are called growth costs because they're spent on growing your business. A look at the income statement of a traditional business shows that you incur sales and marketing costs to bring in revenue for the current period. However, growth costs in subscription service businesses go hand in hand with future ARR. Again, this shows the proactiveness of subscription service business in financial analysis. The sales and marketing expenses you incur this year contribute to the growth in the future ARR.

The sales and marketing costs are taken out of the recurring profit margin. This means that as long as there's growth in the recurring profit margin, you can keep increasing sales and marketing costs. In turn, as you increase the growth costs, you can expect your future ARR to keep climbing up.

Once you subtract growth costs from the recurring profit margin, you remain with net income.

- **ACV**: As explained above, ACV is annual contract value, which is what you expect to earn per subscriber per year. Two elements add to it: upsells or upgrades and new subscribers. Your growth costs are meant to drive upsells and the acquiring of new subscribers. You calculate ACV by dividing the subscriber LTV with the average time a subscriber sticks with you. Let's illustrate what we mean. Suppose that your average subscriber LTV is $15,000 and sticks with you for three years. ACV will be $5,000 ($15,000/3 = $5,000).

When you add the ACV to the net ARR determined above, you get your ending ARR. If you're running your business well, this figure should be higher than the beginning ARR.

The bottom-line is that if you keep the churn rate as low as possible, you can grow your subscription service business fast. On the other hand, if you want to pocket some profits along the way, you'll slow your business growth. It's up to you what you choose, and your circumstances will definitely contribute to your decision-making.

Forecasting Cash Flow in Your Subscription Service Business

At the end of the previous section, we mentioned that your circumstances dictate what you do when your recurring profit margin increases. Before making a decision on the growth of your business, you need to consider how you're going to manage cash flow. The reason this is crucial is that cash is the fuel that makes your business work. For instance, you can't make payroll if you don't have cash. If you're caught with no cash, you might be forced to get a bank loan or investor money as quickly as possible. The possibility is that you might not get any cash that fast. Your best bet is to have cash reserves to use when the need arises.

Before we discuss how to forecast your business's cash flow, let's address this first.

The Meaning of Cash Flow and Why You Need to Forecast It

The basic question to answer before discussing cash flow forecasting is "What is cash flow?" Cash flow is the difference between money that comes in and money that goes out. In short, cash flow = cash in - cash out. If it happens that cash out exceeds cash in, your business is cash flow negative. This is not a great financial position to be in because if you ever need cash quickly, you have to source it from elsewhere. A cash flow position you want all the time is being cash flow positive.

With that said, let's now look at the benefits of having an accurate cash flow forecast.

1. **Reveals future potential cash flow shortfalls**: A cash flow forecast provides you with your cash flow position at some future point in time. If you foresee negative cash flow, you can take steps today to modify your plans or seek funding from investors or banks. Because you'll have the time to do this, you won't have to experience financial stress.

2. **Provides your business's financial health**: What's better than riding a dying horse? It's to dismount it. The same goes if you recognize that your business's financial health is on life support. You can notice this situation provided you conduct an accurate cash flow forecast. With this forecast, you can tell if you're having control over subscriber retention, expenses, and efforts to acquire new subscribers. The good news is that you'll spot these issues many months before they happen and decide what to do about them.

3. **Helps with accurate decision-making**: Your cash flow forecast depends on the inputs you make such as taxes, sales and marketing costs, churn, and COGS. You can play around with these when you pay supplier costs to see what the impact is on cash flow. When you notice that you could potentially land in trouble, you may decide to negotiate with your supplier on payment terms. Another possible scenario is adjusting your growth costs to establish the impact on ARR and cash on hand. Sometimes, you may push hard to grow your business only to place it in a negative cash flow position. Having done cash flow projections, you can decide against aggressively growing your business until it's cash-stable.

4. **Helps identify opportunities for growth**: When we want to grow our businesses, we have a tendency to go online and seeking out other sources to find out what we can do to

achieve that purpose. Sure, we find good ideas that may not necessarily apply to our own situations. Little do we know that we have all the data and information we need to make better growth decisions. For instance, when you've done a cash flow forecast, you may realize that you can improve your offer a bit without running into cash problems. That decision alone can result in improved average revenue per subscriber and boost your future cash flow.

As you can see, there are advantages to performing an accurate cash flow. Why wouldn't you want to do it? By the way, in the process of performing a cash flow forecast, you'll figure out your cash flow statement.

It's time to forecast cash flow. You'll recall that cash flow is about money that comes in versus money that leaves your business. It follows that all we need to create a cash flow forecast are future cash inflows (income) and outflows (expenses)

- **Cash inflows**: This element considers all types of income you expect to receive. The main cash sources for a subscription service business are the following:

  - **Income from the sales of your subscriptions**: This is the primary source of income for your business. It is the top line we discussed under the income statement. On the cash flow statement, you record this income under cash from operations. Only include the cash you receive or deposit in your bank account.

  - **Investments and loans**: Depending on your business goals and the challenges you face, it may be necessary to borrow money from the bank or increase your investment in it. Another source of funding may be an external investment if you deem it necessary. This cash must be included as part of your cash inflows. It's helpful to separate loans from investments when you record these cash sources because you have to repay loans directly. Investments are treated differently.

o **Sales of assets**: Your business will definitely have the equipment you use to operate it. For example, you may have vehicles for traveling to your suppliers. The time comes when you need to replace them and that's when you'll sell the old vehicles. The cash generated forms part of your cash inflows.

o **Once-off fees or sales**: At times, your business may sell some items on a once-off basis. Perhaps you have more inventory than you needed and can't return the items to your suppliers. Your best bet is to make one-time sales. This cash and any one-time fees you charge are added to your cash inflows.

o **Sales tax**: You may be required by your state to charge sales tax, which is the extra money you add to the cost of your products or services. You collect this money on behalf of the state and must hand it over at agreed upon times. Since it comes to your business, it must be included in your cash flow forecast.

o **Interest income**: If you're flush with cash in your bank account, your bank could add interest to that money. For example, if you have $100,000 at the start of a given year and the bank offers 0.23% annual percentage yield (APY), your money will grow to $100,230 ($100,000(1 + 0.23/100) = $100,230) by the end of that year. If you save a lot of money in the bank, this money could be significant. This is income that goes to your cash flow forecast.

When you add together all the above incomes, you wind up with a total cash inflow. This completes one half of estimating your cash flow forecast.

- **Cash outflows**. You can't do every business activity by yourself. You need to have suppliers and perhaps employees, and you have to use many other resources. Many of these resources won't come for free. For example, if you require cloud storage, you'll need to pay a subscription fee probably monthly or annually. You can't run away from spending some of the money you bring into your business. The major expenses to include are the following:

- **Regular business costs**: Expenses to be included in this part are recurring costs such as software subscriptions, payroll, loan repayments, utilities, rent, and other business-related costs.

- **Asset purchases**: We stated earlier that you may need to purchase new vehicles to replace the old ones. Costs associated with this form part of asset purchases. Sometimes, you may want to buy or build your own offices and you should include costs to do so in your cash flow forecast.

- **Taxes**: These expenses include paying the sales tax you collected to the government and income tax if you made a profit. Your income statement will have the data you need to estimate how much income tax you'll need to pay.

- **Non-operating expenses**: Costs in this category include interest payments to make if you've taken out loans. On separate rows, also include any fees incurred, such as those charged by payment processors.

This completes the other half needed to create a cash flow forecast.

The hard work for cash flow forecasting is done when you have your total cash inflows and outflows. What's left is to decide how you're going to approach making your cash flow estimates. The simplest method is the direct approach in which you simply subtract total cash outflows from total cash inflows. However, the direct approach is cumbersome if you have forecast cash flows over long periods of time.

The indirect method comes in handy when forecasting cash flows for short, medium, or long-term periods. Since this approach is a little complex, you can get the services of an accountant to do it for you.

To use this method, you need to use net earnings from your income statement and adjust it for any other income and expenses not included in the income statement. Examples of such cash include cash from investments and loans and depreciation. In the case of non-cash transactions like depreciation, you'll need to add it back to arrive at the accurate cash represented by the net income. You should have a higher net income in the cash flow statement than in the income statement.

The formula for the indirect method is:

Cash flow = net income +/- adjustments

Three Top Tips for Accurate Cash Flow Forecasting

Projecting cash flow can be hard, especially if you've never done it before. It's even more challenging if you're preparing a recurring startup business's cash flow forecast. However, if you implement the three tips provided below, you'll find it a bit easier.

1. **Focus on recording cash, not a sale**. For businesses that sell their services or goods on payment plans, it's easy to confuse cash with revenue. That's why we mentioned above that you should focus on recording revenue that has been registered in your bank account. This means you should adopt cash accounting, not accrual accounting, when forecasting cash flow. This approach avoids having profit and negative or zero cash flow. Make your best estimate for when cash will be in your bank account to make sure your cash flow forecast is accurate.

2. **Understand all your expenses**. To make an accurate cash flow forecast, you can't afford to miss one or two expenses. This means you should have a means of capturing all your business expenses, both operating and non-operating costs. This is where you should find a suitable software, tool, or app that tracks all your expenses. Be careful to select a tool that can work with subscription-type financial data.

3. **Review your cash flow forecasts**. Once you've created a forecast, you'd have completed an important activity. All this work can go to waste unless you use that forecast as a living

document. This means that you regularly compare the actual data against what you forecasted so that you can make timely adjustments to your estimates. The adjustments you make will help you with making new decisions that are likely to affect future cash flow. Most importantly, as you adjust your forecasts, you'll improve how you forecast in the future.

From the discussion above, it's clear that you need to be on top of things in your business: namely cash flow and ARR. Use your income statement to ensure your business is profitable and the forecasted cash flow statement to make sure you never run out of cash.

Checklist

	Go through and ensure you understand an income statement.
	Compare and forecast cash flow.
	Identify growth opportunities.
	Minimize your expenses.

Chapter 9:

Top Five Best Practices of Successful Subscription Service Businesses

Every owner of a subscription service business wants it to be successful. You can cut your learning curve and trial and error if you know what others have done to succeed. Recognizing this, we provide you with five of the top best practices of successful subscription service businesses.

1. Use Storytelling to Illuminate Your Business's Value

You surely want to make as much money as you desire. Persuasion is the name of the game when building a successful subscription service business. Although there are many approaches to persuasion, including delivering quality products or services and providing an excellent subscriber service, few can beat the power of storytelling. You don't have to go far to notice the power of storytelling. Just look at some popular movies and novels. Perhaps consider your own experiences. What movie do you rate as the best of all time? We don't know for sure, but we would venture to say that your pick ticks all the boxes of a good story.

If you're not a movie junkie, perhaps speeches are your thing. Are you familiar with Dr. Martin Luther Jr.'s famous "I have a dream" speech? You probably are because that speech moved many Americans' hearts, including those of politicians. King didn't give a speech: he told a story—the story that gave hope to all kinds of Americans.

Stories can be used in many endeavors, such as in business, to convey messages concisely and clearly. One of its applications is in telling your value proposition to potential and existing subscribers.

The power of a story is in the fact that it elicits emotions—an element necessary to make sales and marketing efforts effective. Our emotions reside in the function of the mind called the subconscious or emotional mind. Since this part of the mind is the most powerful of the two—the other is known as the rational or conscious mind—the buy decision takes place there. However, the rational mind needs facts to justify those emotional decisions we make.

The takeaway is that you should tell business and subscriber success stories. All these must connect with your target audience, which is why knowing them is the bedrock of the success of your subscription service business.

2. Simplify Subscriber User Experience

Imagine this for a moment. You run PPC advertising to send potential subscribers to your business's landing page. Your advertising clicks with potential subscribers and they visit your landing page in throngs. For some reason, no one is entering their contact details in the form. Surprised by the results, you hire a website user experience expert to look at the design of your landing page. Unsurprisingly, they come out with 10 points that are making your landing page ineffective even though they mention that your marketing copy is great. One problem they mention is that your copy is cluttered. The solution is to provide a simple user experience.

Online user experience is a crucial element of success for a subscription service business or any online business.

Both your websites and a subscription app or platform must be welcoming to users. This comes with important benefits for your business, including the following:

- **Increased user interaction**: When your website and software tools are well-designed, they're easy for users to interact with. This means they won't navigate away to competing websites. As a result, users will have pleasant experiences with your brand and will want to interact with your business more. This translates to other benefits, some of which are discussed below.

- **Enhanced subscriber loyalty**: Subscribers who're satisfied with the usability of your tools, products, and service are likely to become loyal and stay for a long time. This will boost your subscriber retention score and increase your MRR and ARR. The bonus is that they may leave glowing reviews about your brand and recommend your subscription service to friends, colleagues, and family members. As a result, your subscriber acquisition costs will be cheaper, which contributes to lower recurring expenses and improved MRR and ARR.

- **Decreased steps for subscribers to find what they want**: Complexity is a deterrent because it makes us think too hard. How many people are willing to do hard thinking? Few, and this isn't good in subscription service businesses. The first law of usability is "Don't make your users think". The processes and experiences with your business should be obvious and self-explanatory, without expecting your customers to do any guesswork.

  Doing so makes it easier for your subscribers to locate what they're looking for. If they look at a web page and are not able to figure out whether something is a button or not, then they'll click the home button of their browser and visit other websites. That's a lost opportunity to turn a visitor into a subscriber or to keep an existing one. Easy navigation makes subscribers think that you have nothing to hide, which enhances your credibility. As you'll recall, this is essential for creating trust—the key to having high subscriber retention rates.

- **Decreased subscriber support expenses**: There's no need for website visitors and subscribers to ask for support if they can easily locate what they're looking for. This means that you won't have to hire too many support personnel or spend a lot of time providing support. As a result, your support costs will decrease, which is good for your subscription service business.

3. Be Willing to Improve Your Business Continually

Why do we have light bulbs in our modern times? Simply because someone, Thomas Edison, was willing to experiment—to run tests. He tested different materials for the filament of his bulbs. Eventually, he came to an idea that worked. Today, we're the beneficiaries of his relentless journey of discovery to invent a working electric bulb. Did you know that you can run similar experiments in your subscription service business?

There are countless elements of your subscription business you can test, including website copy, marketing channels, software tools, offers, pricing, and many more. Sometimes, the test may emanate from the failure of existing approaches while other times you'll run tests to improve current processes.

The starting point of testing is measurements—you need data to spot trends and potential areas that need improvement. For instance, if you notice that your sales letter is converting at X% and similar businesses are converting at higher rates, you should know there's an opportunity for improvement. The challenge is that you won't necessarily hit it out of the park at the first attempt. You'll need to be willing to run tests— sometimes many of them—before you produce desired results.

One of the entrepreneurs who doesn't think twice about trying new things is the cofounder of Paid Memberships Pro, a WordPress platform that helps with starting recurring businesses. Her name is Kim Coleman, a designer and developer. She and her team are obsessed with testing things in her business. For instance, she and her team ran a test in 2016 to test what type of call to action worked best on her landing page. We'll get into how she proceeded with the test and what she found out, but first, let us describe how her landing page looked before the test.

Her landing page featured the main banner that showed a video, a short description of the product, and a button. Visitors who wanted to sign up had to click this button to take the action that the business wanted. The aim of the experiment was to find out which option worked best among the offered alternatives. The three options provided were all linked to the call-to-action button.

To conduct these tests, Coleman needed to run what's known as A/B testing. In this type of testing, you choose one variable to change so that you know what factor produced the results you see. Coleman's test wasn't easy because she had three options to test which gave the best results. The first alternative took visitors who clicked the call-to-action button to a features page, the second sent them to a comparison page of subscriptions, and the third nudged visitors to get started right away with the most popular subscription plan.

When the test results were analyzed, Coleman found out that they converted more users who chose the "Get Started Now" option. Without dillydallying, the company got rid of the two options that didn't do as well. This means that the test revealed a method that could be used to drive more revenue.

As is typical, the test you run will not be the last. The reason is that your business isn't a static entity. It keeps changing or the industry morphs over time. What was once good may become not so good anymore. This means you'll need to run new tests to improve your current results.

Coleman got away with testing three variables because she drove traffic to a single page. Moreover, her test was easier to run on a single page. This may not be the case when you want to test variables such as your landing page's headline or the design of the form. In that case, you'll need to create two landing pages that are similar in all respects, except for the variable you want to test. Instead of sending all your traffic to a single page, you send it to two pages and measure the results. The page that performs best becomes your control—the one that you'll need to beat to generate better results.

Although A/B testing is an advanced technique, we shared it here to make our point about testing clearer.

4. Incentivize Subscribers

We mentioned at the beginning of Chapter 7 that subscription service businesses die or survive based on their subscriber retention. You can't have enough strategies for ensuring that your subscriber retention rate is the highest possible. One method for persuading your subscribers to stick with you is by offering incentives for subscribers who spend more with your business. This will also likely enhance the effectiveness of other subscriber retention strategies, such as loyalty and referral generation.

Subscriber incentives are special rewards granted to subscribers who help you build your brand. For example, you may offer such incentives to subscribers who refer your subscription services to others. Alternatively, you could offer more and better features for subscribers who share their experiences about your business on social media. How you structure these incentives vary based on the type of products on offer. The main aim of subscriber incentives is to convert your subscribers into your marketers.

An example of subscriber incentives is one put into practice by Amora Coffee, a coffee company that offers monthly, bi-monthly, and quarterly subscriptions. At some point, we subscribed to this service and learned about how you may access Amora's incentives. A subscriber had to accumulate a certain number of points to qualify for an incentive. For instance, racking 100 points swung open the opportunity to receive a 20% discount on your next order.

Subscriber incentives are great at building loyalty and subscriber retention. Looking at the above example, a subscriber who wants a 20% discount will have to keep buying to earn points. This means that they'll have to stay a subscriber until such time as they qualify for the incentive. Thus, the program succeeds in retaining a subscriber who might have otherwise canceled their subscription earlier.

Subscriber incentives work because people have a desire to get a deal that's valuable to them. A research study found that incentives, such as discounts, work on both name brand and store brand products. However, customers buy only if their threshold discount is met. In a study it was found that loyalty programs result in increased spending for the majority of customers. Thus, subscriber incentives work, especially if you use a program that resonates with your subscribers.

When offering incentives, you should ensure that the benefits to you exceed the cost. A successful incentive program turns your subscribers into brand ambassadors. It's this effect that leads to free advertising, which in turn, increases brand awareness and leads. Additionally, your brand is likely to stand out from the competing crowd.

If subscriber incentives work so well, how do you create a successful one? The following steps will guide you:

- **Step 1: Understand your subscribers intimately.** Your market research and the data you generate while running your business will be of help when executing this step. The reason for understanding your subscribers is to ensure a subscriber-incentive fit.

- **Step 2: Define your goal for establishing an incentive program.** This is important so that the incentive you select can help drive you toward your goal. Most importantly, goals will help steer your actions and act as a measuring stick to indicate what success looks like.

- **Step 3: Segment your subscribers.** Your subscribers are different and are very likely to respond to incentives differently. Your subscriber research will confirm this. If you have different types of subscribers, you'll need to craft different incentive programs.

- **Step 5: Decide on the structure of your incentive.** Having segmented your subscribers, you'll now design incentives which are likely to work with each segment. Use the interests and behaviors of your subscribers to estimate what type of incentive may work for them. If you aren't clear about this yet, you may run a survey and ask each segment of subscribers what incentive they would like.

- **Step 6: Test your incentives.** It's now time to find out which incentive works best for your subscribers. Testing is necessary so that you don't waste resources on a program that doesn't work. Once you've tested an incentive, you can scale its implementation. Make sure that you track the results to ensure you stay within the incentive budget you have.

- **Step 7: Refine your incentives**. It's possible that your first incentive offer may not work. If this happens, adjust and test again until you find an incentive offer that works. Doing this shouldn't be a problem since by now you should know the importance of innovation and experimentation as discussed elsewhere in this book.

Subscriber incentive programs have been found to work not only by academic researchers, but also by real businesses. A case in point is Uber, the ride hailing company. When it was launching, it crafted an incentive program for riders that helped fuel its growth. Although Uber didn't start as a subscription service, this customer incentive program can be used by such businesses. Uber didn't vet taxi drivers in its initial stages. To attract riders, it incentivized riders by offering them free credits toward future rides for referring their friends. This way, new riders felt comfortable ride hailing even if they knew nothing about the drivers.

Subscriber incentives work when approached with the thought of delivering immense value to subscribers. Consider adding it to your tools for building and growing your business.

5. Promote Your Subscription Services Regularly

If there's one thing that's constant these days, it's noise. Everywhere you look, competitors are trying to outperform your subscription service business. Check your social media feed to gauge how many advertising or promotion messages you receive per day. That's just the tip of the iceberg. If you head over to one of the many blogs in your industry, you're likely to encounter tons of advertisements. All these promotional messages are vying for your attention. Your subscribers are also experiencing what we've just described. How do you stay relevant and competitive in this noisy world?

Promote your subscription services as many times as possible. We see this being modernized in PPC advertising. Many marketers send nearly one email every day either sharing content or promoting their products, including memberships, incentives and more. This is done to stay fresh in the minds of their email subscribers, knowing that when they're ready, they'll buy what is offered if it's the right fit.

You're probably thinking that communicating with your existing and potential subscribers regularly will make them disinterested. Let us ask you a question: Have you subscribed to an email list of a top marketer? We're talking about entrepreneurs who have been in the trenches of online marketing for years. Some of them revolutionized advertising on the internet. If you did, how many emails do you receive from any one of them per week? As for us, we get plenty of their emails each week. Some send emails almost daily. Why? Simply because it works—that is, they make money from doing so.

You can't burn out your audience if you add value to their lives or businesses. It's even better if you can communicate with your subscribers and other audiences through multiple channels such as social media, podcast, email, or even snail mail. Perhaps the simplest channels of communication to use are social media and email. We particularly like email because of the following reasons:

- **It delivers an unparalleled marketing ROI**. A dollar spent in email marketing brings back $42, which is why 47% of marketers prefer it over social media and search engine optimization (SEO). However, you'll need to be adept at crafting messages that win. The good news is that this is a learnable skill. You can use email to provide value-adding content and promotions of things like incentives.

- **Email is great for personalizing messages to recipients**. Personalization is a great tool for getting your emails opened and read. You can personalize emails by including the recipient's name in the subject line as well as in the body of the email. This suggests to the reader that you're talking with them personally, not anyone else. It's partly personalization that makes email effective.

You can imagine how effective your promotions will be when you combine email marketing with social media.

We'd like to clarify what we mean by promotion. Promotion means that you communicate your offer to existing and potential subscribers. However, you still need to follow your sales funnel in order for your promotions to sell. In between promotions, don't hesitate to create and communicate valuable content to your audience. This will help you shorten the lengths of your promotions.

Checklist

	Use storytelling to highlight your value proposition.
	Simplify your users' experience and processes when dealing with your business.
	Consistently tweak and improve your processes and business.
	Provide your customers with incentives.

Conclusion

Subscription services are taking the world by storm. We hope you've made a decision to start yours or convert some of your products or services into subscription services. This book is meant to help you start a successful subscription service business. It's easy to forget what you learned in it if you read it once and put it away. However, there's a shortcut: you can read its summary frequently to improve your understanding of the ideas it shares. Below, you'll find the main ideas you learned.

A subscription service business generates recurring revenue from subscribers, not customers. Subscribers receive a desired service by paying a recurring fee. All kinds of industries are already benefiting from the subscription service business model, including the automobile, airline, education, health, software technology, and retail industries.

Subscription services come with numerous benefits. The top benefit is predictability of revenue, which makes it easy to plan your finances. However, you should retain subscribers for longer to enjoy this benefit. Since it's cheaper to acquire subscribers, your profitability could be higher.

There are three broad categories of subscription service business models: curation, replenishment, and access models. The curation model is the most dominant, followed by the replenishment model, and in last place is the access one. Within these subscription service business models, there are five specific facets. They include the SaaS, e-commerce, on-demand, membership-based, and nonprofit subscription service business models.

- SaaS subscription service model: Subscribers pay a fee in exchange for access to software or software tools. Although it's easier to acquire subscribers, the model is easy to compete with.

- E-commerce subscription model: This uses both the replenishment and curation models. A good example of this model is the subscription box.

- On-demand subscription service model: This is a classic access subscription business model in which subscribers pay a fee to access content when they want. Video has become the preferred mode of content. It can be used in a variety of industries including media and entertainment and the education sectors.

- Membership-based subscription service model: This is where there's content for the public and gated content for paid subscribers. It's an example of the access model.

- Nonprofit subscription service model: This is used by nonprofit organizations to raise donations. This approach works better because recurring donors give four times more than one-off donors.

Like transactional businesses, subscription service ventures can and do fail. Reasons for this vary but the main ones are as follows:

- Lack of innovation, which is not introducing new things. Subscribers get bored and cancel their subscriptions. It's important to inject novelty in your subscription to reduce subscriber cancellations.

- Lack of clarity about target subscriber. Targeting a general subscriber is difficult and costly. The best thing is to focus on a type of subscriber you know intimately in order to be able to sell them your subscription services.

- No mission behind the business. People want more besides products and services. They crave purpose because they have causes they care about.

- Inflexible pricing at the time of subscribing. A single price gives no options and subscribers want alternatives. The problem is that a single price might be too high for your target subscribers, and they won't buy.

- Not involving subscribers. Taking too much time to communicate with subscribers opens a chance for competitors to steal your subscribers. Ask subscribers questions or send them surveys to get them involved.

- Making complex offers. People like simplicity. When what you offer is complex, few people will take the time to try and understand it. Many will switch off and opt for alternatives.

If starting a subscription service business from scratch sounds like a good idea, it's important to know how to do so. It's crucial to follow the right sequence. Here's the process:

- The first action is to find a subscription service business idea.

- Research your market so that you can figure out how best to serve your target subscribers. Researching involves finding out as much as possible about your target subscribers and your competitors.

- Create a subscription product to sell to your potential subscribers. The research above will greatly help with this activity.

- Create a value proposition. Find a reason that will make subscribers want to do business with you instead of your competitors. It should have a potent headline and subheadline.

- Create subscription packages and pricing. You can't price your subscription services any way you wish. The market will guide you. Your pricing strategy might follow the flat, tiered, or hybrid model.

- Select the technology you need. This includes OMS, CMS, marketing automation tools, website, web analytics tools such as Google Analytics and Facebook Pixel, recurring billing system, customer relationship management, and a payment recovery solution.

- Write a sales page to sell your subscription.

- Validate your subscription service business idea.

- Onboard your subscribers.

If you're converting to subscription services, the process you follow doesn't differ much from that of starting from scratch. The difference is that you have existing customers as your target subscribers. You should first figure out why you want to transition to a subscription service business model. When done, evaluate your existing business model and understand your existing customers deeply. Don't forget to study your competition. The rest of the process is similar to what you do when building a subscription service business from scratch.

The easiest method for attracting subscribers to your business is by using the freemium model. Offer something for free to lure potential subscribers. But you should first design and build your sales funnel so that you attract the right potential subscribers. Remember to calculate the conversion so that you can determine the effectiveness of your sales funnel. To convert leads into subscribers, make an irresistible offer—a can't refuse offer.

The key to the success of your subscription service business is subscriber retention. Calculate both the subscriber retention rate and churn rate and monitor them regularly so that you spot issues faster. Strategies to retain subscribers include sending them a newsletter regularly, creating personalized experiences, accepting mistakes, and apologizing quickly.

To measure the success of your business, you need to have financial statements. The most important are the income and cash flow statements. It's crucial to understand terms like ARPU, MRR, and ARR. Remember to forecast cash flows to avoid running out of money to run your business.

The subscription services industry has best practices you can rely on. These include telling stories to communicate the value you offer, running regular promotions, incentivizing your subscribers, simplifying user experiences, and continuous business improvement.

Reviewing this summary will help you refresh what you've learned in this book. Even more importantly, if you share what you've learned with others, the information will stay in your mind longer. One way of sharing what you learned and how you benefited is through writing an Amazon review. Others will thank you for leading them in the right direction when they want to know more about the subscription service business.

Before you go, we just wanted to say thank you for purchasing our book. You could have picked from dozens of other books on the same topic but you took a chance and chose this one. So, a HUGE thanks to you for getting this book and for reading all the way to the end.

Now, we wanted to ask you for a small favor. COULD YOU PLEASE CONSIDER POSTING A REVIEW ON THE PLATFORM? (Reviews are one of the easiest ways to support the work of independent authors.)

This feedback will help us continue to write the type of books that will help you get the results you want. So if you enjoyed it, please let us know!

We wish you much Success on your Journey!

Made in the USA
Columbia, SC
05 January 2025

51272970R00089